Channelizing Self For Success

Dr. Kapil Kakar

DIAMOND BOOKS

ISBN : 978-81-288-3141-6

© Author

Publisher	: Diamond Pocket Books (P) Ltd.
	X-30, Okhla Industrial Area, Phase-II
	New Delhi-110020
Phone	: 011-40712100, 41611861
Fax	: 011-41611866
E-mail	: sales@dpb.in
Website	: www.dpb.in
Edition	: 2011
Printed by	: Adarsh Printers, Delhi- 110032

CHANNELIZING SELF FOR SUCCESS
By - *Dr. Kapil Kakar*

Preface

Often we think of knowing ourselves to the zenith and feel there is nothing more to be known. But a few years down the line we find ourselves smarter and better than before, which suggests that our conception earlier was wrong. This is exactly what this book caters to, what you think about yourself and what you actually are. Believe me there is no magical wand with any successful individual in this world. The charismatic vibrations given by the successful people are due to their understanding about themselves vis-a-vis a particular field.

One often finds that a good businessman or actor need not be a good husband or father. The imperative point here is the question why? Why can't a successful businessman or actor be a good father? It is only because the individual understands himself very well till the time he is a businessman or an actor, but when it comes to becoming a good father and husband, his understanding about himself is very low and his misconceptions about his role of a father or husband are far greater.

This book has been divided into three sections. The first section consists of the quiz, which is self-scoring. It provides you with your current thinking about yourself and life. The second section consists of seven chapters, which caters to the scientific information and methodology of improving the self. Section two is all about providing you with the right tools. Section three is about using those tools in the right direction. Also, it is about using them for much greater cause than only the self.

"Everyone wants to be understood but nobody wants to understand". Think about it and if you realize it, your life can become much better.

I am starting this book with 5 quizzes, which will help you evaluate the self. These quizzes will focus on your fundamentals. Self scoring is part of this quiz that will show you the category which you fall in and why. All this will help you assess the self, so that even without reading the first chapter of the book you take a big leap in knowing the self better.

—*Dr. Kapil Kakar*
Ph.: 9899999158, 65290068
www.kapilkakar.com
www.corporatetrainingindia.net
www.childconfidence.net

CONTENTS

Section - I   7-26
Know Yourself
Quiz

Section - II   27–137
Attitude
1. Understanding the Truth and Your Potential   29–47
2. Positive Learning   48–63
3. Thoughts   64–76
4. Meditation   77–93
5. Forgiveness   94–105
6. Assertiveness   106–125
7. Habits—only strong persons can change them   126–137

Section - III   139–164
Attitude Traits
8. Organisational Skills   141–154
9. Your National Duty   155–164

SECTION - I

Know Yourself
(Self Scoring Quizzes)

QUIZ I

Your belief in destiny?

1. **When you are given a target to achieve :**
   (a) Do you put all your effort and try all good and bad ways to ensure that the target is achieved?
   (b) Do you say, well, if I am destined to achieve it, I will?
   (c) Do you give in your best positively and leave the result to God?

2. **Do you believe in luck?**
   (a) Sometimes   (b) Always
   (c) Never

3. **Do you believe in destiny?**
   (a) Sometimes   (b) Always
   (c) Never

4. **Are marriages made in heaven?**
   (a) No   (b) Yes
   (c) Sometimes

5. **How much control does God/nature have over your life?**
   (a) 25-75%   (b) 50-100%
   (c) None at all

6. **What do you think about astrology?**
   (a) It is a science that can predict your immediate future.
   (b) It is a science that can predict your whole life.
   (c) It is a science that tells you about your actions.

7. **Can astrological solutions change your life for good?**
   (a) Sometimes   (b) Always
   (c) Never

8. Can vastushastra change your future?
   (a) Sometimes   (b) Always
   (c) Never

9. When you are depressed, do you visit astrologers/ vastu consultants?
   (a) Sometimes   (b) Always
   (c) Never

10. Are you confident that their remedies will eliminate your problems?
   (a) Sometimes   (b) Always
   (c) Never

11. Do you think that because of your past actions you are unsuccessful and suffering in this life?
   (a) Sometimes   (b) Always
   (c) Never

12. Do you think that God gives most of the fruits (good or bad) of your actions in this life?
   (a) Sometimes   (b) Never
   (c) Always

Give yourself 5 points for a, 0 points for b and 10 points for c.

0-40 Pts.

It's time to wake up dear. You have surrendered yourself completely to destiny that does not exist. You are always waiting for things to happen and let life take its own course. You believe in waiting for opportunity instead of creating one. You lack initiative, as you believe what has to happen will happen and there is nothing much you can do to be successful and happy. You believe in luck and destiny and forget that God helps those who help themselves. All is not lost yet. Change your attitude and start believing in yourself and in the laws of nature. Work with the laws and not against them. I am sure you don't want an ordinary end to this precious life. Therefore, start moving yourself and get active. You are the master of your own fate. Read the first chapter very carefully. All the best.

45-80 Pts.

You have almost realized that there is no destiny or luck and (a) that you are yourself the master of it. (b) You are on the right path but you have to work on it more quickly and vigorously. You are not quite sure of what you believe in. At times, you feel you are right but at other times, especially when things are not going right for you, you suddenly start feeling that nothing is in your hands. You are close to success, yet far. Stop doubting yourself and your positive thoughts and surrender all your actions to God. Don't expect and run after results. You will see that things will start working for you. To reinforce what you think, start with the first chapter. Believe me, you are almost there. All the best.

85-120 Pts.

Bravo ! You are right there. You have either already started achieving success or you are on the verge of it. Work hard and remain active, don't change your belief. Yes, you are absolutely in the right direction; your belief in-yourself and your actions are commendable. God has given you freedom of performing actions and there is no destiny. You have to make it and you are making it every minute with every thought that you create in your mind, either consciously or unconsciously. You need to introspect by answering the questions and analyzing what you have answered. All the best.

QUIZ II

What do you think and believe about God?

1. **Do you believe in God?**
   - (a) Sometimes
   - (b) Always
   - (c) Never

2. **Do you believe in the laws of nature?**
   - (a) Sometimes
   - (b) Always
   - (c) Never

3. **Do you think that God is biased and partial?**
   - (a) Sometimes
   - (b) Never
   - (c) Always

4. **Do you think accounts maintained by God can ever go wrong?**
   - (a) Sometimes
   - (b) Never
   - (c) Most of the times

5. **Where does God reside?**
   - (a) Specific places like Mathura etc.
   - (b) Everywhere
   - (c) Temples, mosques, churches, and other religious places

6. **Is God full of love?**
   - (a) Sometimes
   - (b) Always
   - (c) Never

7. **Is God involved with what is going on in the universe?**
   - (a) Sometimes attached and at other times detached.

(b) Detached with human activities.

(c) Involved with human activities.

8. **If you pray to God 24 hours a day for material success (say name, fame, money etc) :**
   (a) You will be partially successful in achieving your desire.
   (b) You will be unsuccessful in achieving your desire.
   (c) You will be totally successful in achieving your desire.

9. **What is worship?**
   (a) Both work and prayer is worship.
   (b) Working honestly and dutifully is worship.
   (c) Prayer to God is worship.

10. **During your prayer time, if somebody requests you for help :**
    (a) You will ask him to wait till your prayer is over.
    (b) You will first do his work and pray later.
    (c) You will ask him to come again with an appointment.

SELF-REALIZATION

Give yourself 5 points for a, 10 points for b and 0 point for c.

0-40 Pts.

You have all wrong notions and beliefs about God. Understanding God is the basis of life that unfortunately you disagree with. You think that there is no God and if He exists, He is biased and partial. With this perception, you are certainly taking life and fellow human beings for granted. You think that you can achieve success in your own way and it is useless to follow any laws or principles of nature. Your attitude is to achieve materialistic things. You must substitute competition with co-operation. I have a question for you, who do you think is controlling your involuntary muscles, which work perfectly without you having to interfere? Think about it. 'Better Late than Never'; it is time for you to start thinking in the right way. I suggest you to read the *Bhagwad-Gita* and the *Autobiography of a Yogi* and soon you will start finding peace, prosperity and happiness in life.

45-80 Pts.

You have faith in God but apparently you are not much aware about His laws. You are a good soul with a clean heart. You only lack the real knowledge, i.e., knowledge about God, which you at times want to know but you are careless and lazy and do not take any initiative to know God. As you know, if you do something wrong or right, you are accordingly punished or rewarded by the Laws of Nature. You should try and gain more knowledge as it will enable you to think and decide clearly about your actions. With the kind of knowledge you possess today, it is very hard for you to take decisions and if you take a decision, you also have a feeling of guilt inside you. A little knowledge is dangerous. You are almost convinced that supernatural power will give you what you deserve, as God is impartial. You are a good soul with a clean heart and the only incomplete thing about you is the lack of knowledge, which is because you are careless and lazy at times.

85-120 Pts.

You are on the correct path and sooner or later you, with your dedication, will know more about God. You are one of the few out of the millions who not only believe in God but also want to get to the ultimate truth. All you have to do is to continue moving on this path and sooner or later you will realize God. As you have already realized, the laws of nature are just and fair and whatever an individual is today, he himself is responsible for that state of life. Man has created and keeps creating good and ugly circumstances for himself in life through his actions. You should keep your head straight and move forward as your concepts about life are largely right. Make an effort to clear your remaining doubts, so that you can be nearer to the truth. Keep your interest and inquisitiveness about god and nature alive as this is your only permanent and true home; the rest is temporary.

QUIZ III

How much do you know about mind?

1. How much role does the mind play in your success if you constructively use it?
    - (a) 75-100%
    - (b) 50-74%
    - (c) 25-49%
    - (d) 1-24%
2. How much of the mind does a human being use in his life?
    - (a) Below 10%
    - (b) Between 10% - 50%
    - (c) Between 50% - 75%
    - (d) Above 75%
3. Do you think our minds are interconnected?
    - (a) Yes
    - (b) No
    - (c) Sometimes
4. Do you believe in the power of thought that comes from your mind?
    - (a) Yes
    - (b) No
    - (c) Sometimes
5. Can positive thoughts change your life?
    - (a) Yes
    - (b) No
    - (c) Sometimes
6. Where are your thoughts processed?
    - (a) Subconscious mind
    - (b) Conscious mind
    - (c) Unconscious mind
7. If you see a person with a good personality in a party —

(a) Will you envy him?
(b) Will you be jealous and indifferent to him?
(c) Will you observe his positive qualities and inculcate them in your life?

8. **If you are invited for a party where people who are invited love to hate —**
    (a) Will you attend that party sullenly?
    (b) Will you enjoy that party down to the wire?
    (c) Will you make an excuse and not go there?

9. **Are you moody?**
    (a) Never   (b) Always
    (c) Sometimes

10. **Do you like making friends?**
    (a) Always   (b) Never
    (c) Sometimes

11. **Do you like your peers and relatives?**
    (a) Always   (b) Never
    (c) Sometimes

12. **When you find something tempting —**
    (a) Do you ensure that you have it though you cannot afford it?
    (b) Do you forget about it completely if you cannot afford it?
    (c) Though you don't buy is it always on your mind?

0-40 Pts.

You don't give any importance to the mind and thoughts. Apparently, you have no knowledge about the mind and its activities. My dear friend, if you don't start concentrating on your mind and your thoughts, then very soon you will be leading a negative life. You possess a lot of anger, jealousy, hatred, envy for others. The worse is that you are convinced that the way you think and act is the right way as the people around you are all wrong with no understanding of life. You are an egoist and you feel happy about this. People are afraid of you· as they don't want to interact with you and you take this as respect given by them to you. Start taking your mind seriously by observing the thoughts that come in it. Eliminate the negative thoughts from your mind and embrace positive ones. If you don't do this, you will not change positively as a person. Love others and find the best in others.

45-85 Pts.

You have some knowledge about the mind and you recognize the importance of the positive mind and positive thoughts. You, at times get moody, selfish and even jealous and are confused. You also lack concentration and discipline. This also affects your decision-making as you are unsure about what is the right decision. You also think too much about your decisions. Be determined to minimize if not throw all these negative emotions out. Though you have an idea about the mind, don't be complacent, as you still have to know more. And also practice more to achieve good, noble, positive thoughts, which will eliminate your restlessness, anxiety, strain and anger and will bring you closer to peace and prosperity. Keep on making a conscious effort about your thoughts by eliminating the negative ones till the time it becomes a habit.

90-120 Pts.

You have good knowledge about the mind. Maintain it. You have successfully crossed the first step but this should not make you complacent. Your knowledge is of no use if you don't apply it with determination and success. You know the importance of positive thinking and it is the mind that initiates you into action.

Answers
Q1 & 2 : a -10, b - 5, c - 0
Q 3 - 6 & Q 9 - 11 : a - 10, b - 0, c - 5
Q 7 : a - 5, b - 0, c - 10
Q 8 : a : 0, b - 10, c - 0
Q12 : a - 0, b - 10, c - 0

QUIZ IV

Your Discriminative ability

1. **Do you believe this world is working in a synchronized and logical manner?**
   (a) Always   (b) Sometimes
   (c) Never

2. **Do you believe that you are responsible for every cause and effect that affects your life?**
   (a) Always   (b) Sometimes
   (c) Never

3. **Your servant is cleaning your room/ house. Do you ensure that you always keep an eye on him so that he does not steal anything?**
   (a) Never   (b) Sometimes
   (c) Often

4. **Do you supervise over your subordinate to see whether he is doing his work properly or not?**
   (a) Often   (b) Sometimes
   (c) Never

5. **Do you start criticizing/ agreeing about someone just by listening to one side of the story?**
   (a) Never   (b) Sometimes
   (c) Often

6. **Do you think God is enjoying this big earthly drama by creating misunderstanding among people?**

(a) No (b) At times
(c) Yes

7. **Do you think anger is always wrong?**
   (a) No (b) At times
   (c) Yes

8. **If you see someone littering on the road or driving rashly, do you mention this in general as and when you get a chance to do so?**
   (a) Never (b) Sometimes
   (c) Often

9. **Is taking a decision from your heart good?**
   (a) Never (b) Always
   (c) At times

10. **Is evil a part of God or a separate entity, which is fighting with God for supremacy?**
    (a) Part of God (b) A separate entity

11. **With what thought process do you conduct actions in life?**
    (a) "You win I lose" (b) "You lose I win"
    (c) "I win you win"

12. **Can one be successful without being clever and diplomatic in life?**
    (a) Yes (b) No

13. **Is God broadminded? (Reply, keeping in mind that religions are supposed to be conservative, orthodox and messengers and reflection of God?)**
    (a) Yes (b) No

14. **Should rules, regulations, laws and principles change with the era even though they might represent the opposite?**
    (a) Yes (b) No

15. **If you deprive your spouse of sex, and if he/ she**

involves in pleasure with someone else, do you think it is a sin?

(a) No   (b) Yes

Give yourself a-10, b-5, c-0 for Question Nos. 1, 2, 3, 4, 5, 6, 7, 8.

Give yourself-a-10, b-0 for Question Nos 10, 12, 13, 14, 15.

Give yourself- a-0, b-0, c-10 for Question Nos 9, 11.

0-50 Pts.

Your discriminative ability is highly principled and orthodox, which has a very stringent unflexible view about life and God. You are not ready to listen to the opinion of others but believe in imposing your opinion like a dogmatic teacher who believes that what he does and thinks is right and the rest is all wrong. Also, if you look deep inside your heart and intellect, you will acknowledge that there are so many questions that remain unanswered and actually haunt you. Unfortunately, they have been put by you in cold storage conveniently. Your decisions in life have been hasty and self-centred as you thought this was the best way to live your life. You seriously need to overhaul your discriminative ability not on the basis of what has been said and written but purely on the basis of relieving your experiences in thoughts and measuring the outcome. Please remember, "Human accounts can go wrong but God's accounts can never go wrong".

55-110 Pts.

You are confused. Your heart says something and your mind says something totally different. You tend to brood over things for too long and your discriminative faculty varies, in the sense that at times, your discriminative faculty is excellent and at other times it is very bad. This may be due to lack of knowledge and wisdom that helps in discriminating between good and bad. You should spend time reading good knowledgeable books that enhance your intellect and make you feel more assertive and confident about your decision-making ability. After all, good or bad decision making is highly dependent on good or bad discriminative faculty.

115-150 Pts.

Your discriminative faculty is excellent. What you have to see is whether you are near your destination or not. So near yet so far. What is meant here is whether you apply/implement what your discriminative faculty suggests to you, or, are there lots of materialistic temptations that keep alluring you away from your correct thoughts? You have reached a stage where implementation can merge you with God. Surely you must have done a lot of thinking, reading and at times, writing before coming to this excellence of discrimination between good and bad.

QUIZ V

Your Faith in God?

How do you/ would you react/contemplate :—

1. **After doing your work properly, are you anxious about the outcome of your work?**
   (a) Often (b) Sometimes
   (c) Never

2. **Do you think about people whom you see enjoying life that according to you, they don't deserve?**
   (a) Often (b) Sometimes
   (c) Never

3. **Do you believe some people are luckier than others ?**
   (a) Often (b) Sometimes
   (c) Never

4. **Do you believe in God?**
   (a) Never (b) Sometimes
   (c) Always

5. **Do you think your boss has prejudice for/against people in your organisation?**
   (a) Often (b) Sometimes
   (c) Never

6. **When in trouble, does the thought of and the act of surrendering to God come to you?**
   (a) Never (b) Sometimes'
   (c) Often

7. **Do you believe in the Laws of Nature?**
   (a) Never   (b) Sometimes
   (c) Always

8. **When in difficulty, do you think God loves you?**
   (a) No   (b) Probably
   (c) Yes

9. **You are on your way to your office and you feel that your boss will scold you unnecessarily for something that you have not done. How would you feel?**
   (a) Overwhelmed with fear
   (b) Nervous
   (c) Confident

10. **Your loved one has done a terrible wrong, would you—**
    (a) Hope that he does not get caught
    (b) You will be sure that he being smart and you being there to help him out, he will not get caught.
    (c) You will be sure that in spite of your and his best efforts, he will get caught.

11. **Do you think God is biased/partial?**
    (a) Always   (b) Sometimes
    (c) Never

12. **Someone comes and humiliates you for something that you have not done, and you could not react at that time...**
    (a) Will you take the initiative of teaching him a lesson?
    b) Would you hope he is punished?
    (c) You would just sit back and watch what happens to him.

Give Yourself- a-0, b-5, c-10 for Question Nos 1-7 & 9, 11, 12.

Give Yourself a-0, b-0-, c-10 for Question Nos. 8 & 10.

0-35 Pts.

It seems you don't believe in the existence of good and bad or you are self-centred individual who thinks about himself always and has no particular concern about others. On the contrary, you are a student of science who does not believe in anything other than what exists. But here, we will focus on the former case because most of the people are not associated with that deep scientific research and background. You are only concerned with people who can help you accumulate monetary success because you believe that only materialistic life is important since it can be seen and experienced. One should concentrate on that instead of wasting his/her time on metaphysical subjects. Also your family/ friend atmosphere combined with your own experiences suggests to you that taking care of oneself is the main goal of life. But please go back to your experiences and try to see them from another angle : that if those experiences have occurred with you, how were your previous actions wrong. Don't justify yourself but just be critical about the self and see. If your belief is based on the other experiences, then my friend, I will want you not to believe in them because they will narrate only their side of the story. Start having faith in God and His Laws and the best way to start doing it is with meditation. Don't compel yourself to have faith in God but at the same time start pondering over your existence, death, and meditative experience. All the best...

40-80 Pts.

Confused, confusion, confused ... this is what happens more often than not with you. At times you start believing in God with full devotion and also have tears rolling down your eyes when you thank Him for what He has done for you. At other times, you start questioning his existence critically. In both cases, you must comprehend that your extreme reactions are not based because of God but the results that are bestowed upon you. Hence, you should firmly and consistently start having full faith in God instead of confusing yourself all the time and crying and apologizing about it later. Be a man with consistent thoughts rather than an erratic individual whose thoughts can change at any time for good or bad due to experience. Don't try sailing in two boats at the same time. You will have to start practicing detachment from the results of your action with a firm belief that "You get what you deserve" and "The Laws of Nature are the same for every one of us" and "God's accounts can never go wrong". Do not let your circumstances and experiences affect your faith. Instead ponder over your actions that have led to those experiences.

85-120 Pts.

There is nothing much to say to you as you must have already started feeling infinite experience and connection with God, which makes you reiterate about His Laws and Existence that are as real as you. You just have to continue believing in Him and yourself and as politicians say *dilli door nahin* (Delhi is not far off) and for you the final destination and complete joy and bliss, which is already there will only increase with time and take you to eternity.

I am starting this book with 5 quizes which will help you to evaluate the self. These quizes will focus on your fundamentals. Self-scoring is part of this quiz which shall come along the category which you fall in and why. All this will help you to assess the self, so that even without reading the first chapter of the book you take a big leap in knowing your self better.

SECTION - II

ATTITUDE
(Self-Analysis Tips and Techniques for Improvement)

Chapter 1

Understanding the Truth and Your Potential

Twins Experience

There were twins in Kavita's womb. As their consciousness grew, they were happy that they were alive. One of them said, "Is it not great that we are alive?"

The twins started developing and observing the changes happening in them as they grew. One of the twins exclaimed, "What is happening to us?"

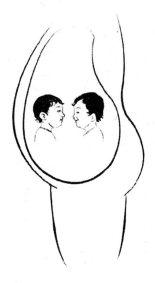

The other said, "I suppose our stay in this universe is coming to an end".

"But I don't want to die, I wish I can stay here always," said one.

"But we are helpless, nothing is under our control, we have no choice," said the other. "But maybe, there is life after death."

"But how can that be?" exclaimed one. "We will lose our breath and how can life be possible without it? Besides, we have seen evidence that others were here before us, and none of them has returned to tell us there is life after death. No, this is the end. Maybe there is nothing after all."

"But there must be something more and meaningful than this," said the other. "Otherwise how could we have got in here? How could we remain alive?"

"Have you ever seen our creator?" said one.

"May-be she lives only in our minds. May-be we made her up because the idea made us feel good."

So the last days in the womb were filled with deep questioning and fear.

Finally, the moment of birth came. When the twins had passed from their world, they opened their eyes and cried with joy - for what they saw exceeded their fondest dreams.

This is birth ... and that was death.

Message

Like the twins, we all think that now it's all over for us, we have come to a dead end and now there is no way out. And we think about this dead end so many times in our lives but every time we invariably find a solution. Don't we? Yes, we always get a solution especially when we are least expecting it.

Right from childhood when we had our first interaction with studies we found it scary, as we never thought life was about learning. We always thought it was more about enjoying. When we grew a little older we realized that we are tested by the world whether or not we have understood the learning properly. When we grow a bit older, we start realizing the expectations our school, friends, parents and teachers have from us. And with each year adding to our lives, we have more and more expectations from ourselves, what subjects should I choose; what are the other alternative streams I have; which courses are in demand and why? And then we start our career, get married, have children... and life goes on, threatening us most of the times with dead ends but we always manage to survive them, at times even without a scratch.

We should realize that there is nothing as an end. And we have seen it through the story as well. What can be the purpose of life if it has an end? The life, its meanings and its temporary solutions will otherwise seem futile and depressing and we keep living with the illusions about end as if they were the only reality. But that end never comes. We fear the end but the end never comes.

Similarly, our efforts never go waste. No matter what we think, how we think and what we do, where there is an effort, there is a proportionate result. I understand that this is hard to believe. Your friends in school must have told you umpteen times that they don't study much, or your colleagues in the office must have often given you the picture that they get promotions or success not because they work harder but because they know how to handle the boss. At times, you also tend to follow in their footsteps by not studying hard and working well, but still you find success alluding you and helping your peers. As they reiterate that they never studied or always knew the boss's mood and acted accordingly. In fact, whatever they studied they got in the question paper or you criticize yourself for not handling the boss well and eventually you tend to blame it on luck.

In my workshops, I generally ask what percentage of a role does luck and hard work play in our lives. And the answer that I get varies from 10:90 in favour of luck or 90:10, or 50:50 or 70:30 etc.

Channelizing Self for Success   *31*

My next question to them is what do you understand by luck and hard work. For me, hard work is when we work towards something sincerely using all our resources and potential to achieve our targets. And the results that we achieve are in proportion to it whether we like it or not. We all realize that efforts are in our hands but not the results. The second question is what is luck? For me, luck is when you get something that you don't deserve in comparision to the efforts put in. To elucidate, if you see your friend working hard and you find that he has failed or just passed, you would exclaim bad luck or hard luck because you and your friends thought that he did not deserve it. Similarly, when you see someone not working hard in life and still being successful, you tend to say it is his good luck. And funny Hindi statements start flowing like *jab samay balwan, gadha pahalwan*, i.e., when time is on your side nothing can stop you, but are these statements true? Let us analyze it more closely.

In our Indian culture, our upbringing is such that almost all the Indians believe that their fate has already been decided by God and nothing is in their own hands. That is why statements like *daane daane per likha hai khane wale ka naam, hum apni zindagi likhawa ke ate hain* or *jo hona hai vo to ho kar hi rahega* etc. are often used. Also in mythological serials played on television we see Narad Muni approaching Lord Krishna who is seated somewhere in the clouds and Naradji asks "*hai prabhu ab apki agli lila kaun si hai*". Then we have bhajans like *hey ram, hey ram "tu hi bigade tu hi savare"* and people pray with the hope that since nothing is in their hands, hence, God will bless them and eliminate all their miseries and replace them with happiness.

Let us Brainstorm of what has been said above.

The above example triggers the thought process that whatever good or bad is happening in their life, is all because of God and they tell their spouses and children that they should not be held responsible for the failures in their lives. Hence, we Indians have a very nice way of washing our hands off our responsibilities.

The majority of people blame God for their failures and sufferings. They firmly believe in luck, fate, destiny etc. They even curse God for their sufferings. But is there really something as fate or destiny? I would not only say that there is nothing such as luck but also say that there is nothing as fate or destiny too, or nothing is predestined as many people think it to be.

Imagine a person is suffering in life, i.e., he is surrounded by tension, ill-health, failure, bankrupcy etc., or is living a successful, happy and wealthy life having everything that he desires for. In both the cases if he is destined to live as he is presently living, there has to be some logic behind it. Since everything in this world is based on logic and intelligence. That is why there is a reason behind every muscle whether voluntary or involuntary. Everything has a function based on logic. That is why we see everything happening in this world with perfection. We don't hear that today one planet has overtaken the other planet or of planets changing their orbits. Everything in this world is working in a synchronized manner and that is the reason we don't have to make our liver, lungs, heart etc. function as they are already working perfectly for us.

Even doctors and scientists acknowledge the fact that whether it is the body or the earth, every part has a meaning attached to it. Imagine, if our feet are replaced by our head and our head by our feet then how will one be able to view the sky or how will the blood circulate in the body. The menstrual cycle that females have every month also has a logic and if this would not have happened, there would have been a major health problem to the ladies. Whatever goes in our body also comes out. This shows our body is not a storehouse which defies logic but a logically well made structure.

Going back to the beginning of our discussion about luck, fate, as I can understand, one logic can be that there is no logic. Surprised! By this I mean that if we assume, that all our births, our struggles, our successes, and our failures have been at the mercy of God, it would mean that whatever we have got so far or will get further in life has been created by God. He has made us all puppets in His hands and is playing with us all the time at, His convenience and pleasure, without us really doing anything independently. Like the word pre-destiny which means that the things will happen the way they are supposed to happen, then my next question is, what is God getting out of all this drama when He destines a soul to be rich or poor, happy or sad, successful or failure etc., without the soul deserving it ? Think about what He is getting from all this, where and whenever He wants He punishes the soul and whenever He wants He rewards the soul. This suggests that God works on mood swings. There is no such thing like karma and rewards for the soul. This clearly means God is biased; He is partial and moody as whatever results he wants to bestow on humans, he gives without evaluating. This is something seen mostly in movies when a cunning king or a rich man treats an ordinary man like an insect and rewards or punishes him with riches or death. And all this happens according to his mood or whichever way he feels pleased without the ordinary man deserving either of the two.

Secondly, we can have yet another logic, which apparently is more convincing. Some people believe that our present life is destined as per our previous actions. They say the actions performed in the previous birth, the result of those actions whether good or bad has been destined in this birth. If you ponder over this, my question to you would be, 'How do we know that whatever we are doing today is the result of our previous actions in past birth or this birth is given to us to perform actions (karma) and the next birth would be destined'. As a believer of destiny that means you will not be performing good/bad actions in your present life. How do you and I know, that the present birth has been given to us to perform actions or are results of our previous birth?

Nature or God, whatever you may call it, who is running this world so perfectly and impeccably, how can He make such a blunder? At least, I cannot digest that Nature has given mind and intelligence to us to understand everything except that whether this life has been given to man to perform actions or is he there to redeem the fruit of actions of the previous birth? I am sure you would agree it is contradicting the whole thing. I can assure you that nothing in this world is contradiction or coincidence or luck. I would like you to read this again and again till you are able to comprehend these self-created complicated theories of some fellow-human beings. If you can understand this, you will know and recognize your purpose of life that will get you closer to peace and happiness that everyone strives for.

Strangely and sadly enough, we have audio and video cassettes being made about God controlling us and making our destiny but in the Bhagvad Gita, the Lord has clearly given these magical tips.

In Text 9 Ch. 9 the Lord Says: " *All this work cannot bind me. I am ever detached from all these material activities, as if neutral*".

In Text 29 Ch. 9 the Lord says: " *I envy no one, nor am I partial to anyone. I am equal to all. But whoever renders service unto me in devotion is a friend, is in me and I am also a friend in him*".

In Ch. 5 Text 15, the Lord says: " *Nor does the supreme Lord assume anyone's sinful or pious activities. Embodied beings, however, are bewildered because of ignorance, which covers the real knowledge*".

The above text clearly proves that God is impartial. Therefore, God is not dictating you to do anything as per his wishes. He is simply observing each one of us and accordingly awarding the soul. He is detached and beyond material activities. In text 29, He talks about devotion but devotion does not mean that you become a saint and leave your family and friends. You can show your devotion by doing your prescribed duties towards your family and work. In the Bhagvad Gita, the Lord has said that if you do not perform your duties, you will incur sin. In Text 5, the Lord has clearly said that He does not create any situation for anybody, we do it for ourselves.

Therefore, make and feel yourself responsible for your own act. Don't conveniently put the blame on God. "You get what you deserve and not what you want". Tell yourself you are a child of God and God has nothing against you. Start taking initiative and overcome fears that are the obstacles of life. Have faith in God and His Laws.

Why should we do right things in the right way?

I am sure that after analyzing whatever is said and written let us try and get into how we generally behave in our lives and is doing so correct. It is easy to get excited and do wrong things. We tend to do it because we enjoy doing it, we find it easy and we see the opportunity of availing instant success and hence, we say to ourselves, " Why should we not do it" "If I don't do it, someone else will do it"; or "If I don't do it what will my friends think about me"; or "I have seen so many people doing wrong in life yet I find them happy and flourishing", "My friends say that they don't study and still they come out with decent results and I, who slogs so hard still manage only to pass..." and it goes on and on.... . and we come with myriad of reasons for not doing the right things in the right ways.

The first question we should ask ourselves is why should I do right things and why not wrong things in the right way? To elucidate, why should I waste my time studying hard when my friends are trying to get the question paper leaked, why should I not also try to get it out with them? Why should I waste my time in giving interviews and not work to get the right contact/ approach? Why should I tell the truth to the customer? Why not spin him so that he gets confused and convinced about my product at the same time?

We will like to do the easier things in the above cases because it is simple and we feel that it almost comes quickly with assured results. And we have always been falling in the same traps though the situations and circumstances are invariably different. When we graduate from school to college, we again work in the same way and look out for things to run our lives smoothly. So we choose for doing the wrong thing in the right manner.

I can end this with another story about how oblivious we are most of the time and we only tend to realize when the suffering is already befallen us.

Fish experience

Two fish, swimming in the river, saw a piece of bread dangling before them. As the younger fish moved toward it with an open mouth, the older fish cried out, "Stop! You can't see it, but there is a hook inside that bread. It is connected with an invisible line to a pole outside the water. There is a man holding the pole. And if you eat the bread, the hook will get caught in your jaw and the man will pull you out of water. He will cut you open with a knife, roast you on a fire and eat you." The young fish stopped.

And the two of them swam away. But when the young fish was alone, it thought, "Let me investigate for myself how accurate these claims are." She went back to the piece of bread, swam around it, above and below it. After a long search, she said to herself, "I've looked far and wide and I haven't found any sign of a man, a pole, a

knife, of a fire. In fact, I've found no trace of anything outside this water we live in. These must be just stories." It went back to the bread and ate it. The hook caught in its jaw, it felt being yanked out of the water and saw a pole, a man and a knife, but at that point its knowledge was useless.

Message

Do the right things and not the wrong things right, otherwise you will be like the helpless fish, who would beg for some magic to happen to save her life but by that time it might be too late.

How do things work and happen?

This question is not as difficult as it sounds. Science and technology, inventions and discoveries have answered many unbelievable questions. No matter how complicated a quary may be, if not all, most of them can be answered with proficiency. Let me share a couple of stories with you, which, if you understand, there will be nothing left for you to doubt Nature.

Ramlal's experience with God

Ramlal prays for two hours everyday in the morning before going to office. The omnipotent and omnipresent God answers to his prayer by giving/adding 500 points to his Balance Sheet. God says in this era/yuga where I see not many people have time for me even for a minute; or if people do remember me they do it for 5-10 minutes; and here you are remembering me for 2 hours every day hence, you deserve 500 points. Now Ramlal, when he gets up from his two hours long puja is found screaming at his servant saying, "Where are my clothes you fool?" and omnipresent God takes away 50 points for his bad behaviour and now Ramlal's Balance Sheet reads 450 points. Then there is a phone call and Ramlal tells his wife to lie that he is not at home. God further takes away 100 points as he finds Ramlal troubling somebody. Hereafter, Ramlal goes to the office and continues doing evil, selfish deeds and breaking promises and commitments and at the end of the day God takes away 700 points from him. Hence, the Balance Sheet now reads negative (–) 200 points. And Ramlal exclaims, questioning the existence of God, by saying, "God, do you actually exist or not? The first thing in the morning after bathing I worship you for 2 hours everyday. Forget sustaining me and realizing my submissions, you have further deteriorated by wealth, health and happiness." Ramlal does not realize that reasons for his downfall in life are his actions and not God as He is impartial and His accounts never go wrong.

Message

Trust God and His Laws. They are equal for all of us. His laws do not make mistakes but our perceptions, being selfish, make mistakes in analyzing it. Hence, we should question ourselves rather than questioning the Laws of Nature.

Ramlal and Shyamlal's experience with destiny

Ramlal and Shyamlal were the best of friends. Both bachelors, working in the same organization as colleagues, used to spend most of the time together whether at office or at home. As their views on life were identical, their actions typically followed their views. Together they used to spoil the office environment by ridiculing and making fun of others, delaying work, troubling others, and taking bribe. At home, they were found mostly in a drunken state. Being firm believers of astrology they both went together to a Swami and requested him to tell their future. Swamiji on their request predicted their date of death, which was exactly five months away.

For the first time, both the friends reacted in a different manner after hearing the news. Ramlal said, "Since I am about to die why not enjoy my life to the fullest?" and he started boozing, womanizing etc. Shyamlal, contrary to his friend, said, "Since I am about to die after some time, I will concentrate and worship God as I will be with Him shortly." So he started praying, helping others, and learning about God. After three months Ramlal expired, two months earlier than predicted by Swamiji. Shyamlal continued working, surrendering his actions to God and counting days for his death. Five months passed by and nothing happened to Shyamlal. Then another month passed by and he was in perfect state of health. Once again he approached swamiji and told him that his prediction of the timing of death was totally wrong, as his friend had expired two months earlier than the day of prediction and he was still alive.

To this swamiji answered, "You both reacted differently to the news of your death. What I predicted was not wrong but you both acted differently. Had you both continued to live the same life that you were living then you would have died exactly at the time I told you, i.e., after 5 months. But the two of you took this news with different perception. Ramlal accelerated on his wrong actions and death came to him early whereas you applied brakes on the earlier actions and you started living a changed lifestyle of a responsible and good individual. Hence, your actions got you away from the jaws of death."

Message

We are responsible for our actions and our actions are responsible for the kind of life we live, or rather how life treats us. If we try to play smart with the Laws, they reciprocate by playing a smarter one on us with the results we deserve. We get what we deserve and not what we desire.

Don't worry. Whatever time you have taken in learning about life will not go waste as nothing goes waste in this world. This chapter was very essential for discussion because now I believe I am addressing this book to someone who believes in introspections and corrections and not on fate and destiny.

After going through all these examples and experiences, there is one good news that I want to share with you, reiterate and substantiate whatever I have said. Often people say that this world is bad because it is *kali yuga* and things will remain bad in the near future also till this *yuga* finishes. And this is a very vocal excuse to criticize each and every one and comfortably say that things are bad. Let us get back to some logic and see whether we are evolving or going from bad to worse. If we are evolving then how is it possible that we are living in *Kali yuga*, the Dark Age. How can anyone evolve in a Dark Age? How is it that the standard of living of the people worldwide is getting better and better? How has astronomy advanced so much in the last few hundred years? How can the rich and famous westerners get attracted to spirituality, Kumbh Mela, meditation and vegetarianism to name a few? Why is it that motivators of today also speak about spirituality? Why do we see more and more people, whether rich or poor, approaching and following gurus? Don't all these trends show that we are moving towards God? If that is so, then how is it possible in *Kali Yuga*.

Needless to say, *Kali Yuga* is supposed to be the worst of the four *Yugas*. The human intellect is only one fourth developed and he cannot grasp anything beyond the gross material creation. The best is *Satya Yuga* in which man can comprehend, even God and the spirit beyond the invisible world. *Satya Yuga* is followed by *Treta Yuga*, then comes *Dwapara Yuga* and finally *Kali Yuga*. The general impression among Hindus world-wide is that we are in Kali Yuga. But Sri Sri Swami Yukteswar Maharaj Ji (1855-1936) the guru of Parmahansa Yogananda Ji (the author of *Autobiography of a Yogi* and the founder of Yogoda Satsang Society, which mainly operates from Ranchi and America) had a different opinion. He was a self-realized Swami who took Samadhi in 1936.

The general understanding is that *Satya Yuga* is for 17,28,000 years, *Treta Yuga* is for 12,96,000 years, *Dwapara Yuga* is for 8,64,000 years and *Kali Yuga* is for 4,32,000 years. Swami Sri Sri Yukteswar Maharaj had said that there was a story behind the above mentioned figure and he has also described, by mathematical calculation, where these figures went wrong.

The calculation mistake started during the reign of Raja Parikshat, just after the completion of *Dwapara Yuga*. At that time Maharaja Yudhisthira, noticing the appearance of the dark *Kali Yuga*, gave his throne to his grandson, Raja Parikshat. Maharaj Yudhisthira, together with all the wise men of his court went to the Himalayas. Thus, there was no one left in the court of Raja Parikshat, who could understand the principle of correctly calculating the ages of several yugas. Hence, after the completion of *Dwapara Yuga* nobody dared to make the introduction of Kali Yuga. Therefore the first year of Kali Yuga was numbered along the age of *Dwapara Yuga*. After many years the wise men of that time realized that the period of *Kali Yuga* is 1200 years. But as their intellect was not suitably developed, they came to the conclusion that these 1200 years of Kali Yuga were not the ordinary years of our earth but were the years of the Gods consisting of 12 months and 30 days in each month. And each God day was equal to one year on earth. Going by this-

$$1 \text{ Day} = 1 \text{ year}$$
$$360 \text{ days} = 360 \text{ years}$$

Satya Yuga : 360 years × 4800 years = 17,28,000 years
Treta Yuga : 360 years × 3600 years = 12,96,000 years
Dwapara Yuga : 360 years × 2400 years = 8,64,000 years
Kali Yuga : 360 years × 1200 years = 4,32,000 years.

He further stated that out of 4800 years of *Satya Yuga* (400+4000+400) the four hundred years before and after *Satya Yuga* are the cusp. Similarly 3600 (300+3000+300), 2400(200+2000+200) and 1200(100+1000+100) before and after of *Treta, Dwapara* and *Kali*, respectively, are cusp also. His calculations further indicate that in 1600 AD, the *Kali Yuga* (the last 100 years of Kali Yuga were cusp as explained earlier) so the characteris-tics of *Dwapara Yuga* also started coming into force. And in 1600 AD,

William Gilbert discovered magnetic forces. In 1609, Kepler discovered the Law of Astronomy and Galileo produced a telescope. In 1670, Newton discovered the Law of Gravitation. And in 1899 the cusp of 200 years of *Dwapara Yuga* was also completed. Now we are in the Full *Dwapara Yuga* and that is the reason man has taken a big leap in the last hundred years.

If you look at human history of the last two thousand years, man had only indulged in wars, captivity, disrespect to fellow human beings, specially women, working undemocratically etc. But definitely in the last five hundred years, each day man seems to be evolving. He has started following democratic processes worldwide. The disrespect for fellow human beings, though not vanished, but is much less. Men and women are at par. Emotions of others are respected more than ever. When Maharaji had revealed this calculation in AD 1894, he called it 26th *Falgun*, 194 *Dwapara*.

Hence, your potential is in your hand

Yes, believe this or not, in this age of grooming, you can certainly improve the look of a person but can you change people's personalities also at the same time? Certainly not. You may be able to groom one person in one year and the other individual may take three years to reach where the first person reached in the first year. Hence, we have to acknowledge the importance of constructive time in becoming what we want to become. And for that, it becomes imperative for each one of us to know our interest and skills, so that we use the time in enhancing already what we are good at and do not take up something just because others are doing well in it or because your friends have taken it up.

We all have equal potential but in different fields or activities. And it is that potential which has to be identified, accepted, and moved on with. This is very important. One often hears that he has better potential than the other. This may be true in a given field. But in some other field, the not so potential individual may show better results. So, if people tell you that you don't have potential or have an outstanding potential, don't listen to them and move on. But if eighty per cent people agree that you don't have potential, then it is surely time for you to think and see what and how you can do something about it.

Solutions to enhance potential may differ from individual to individual, but one thing is for certain : the solution exists and it works like a medicine to a patient. Like disease is temporary and it is cured through medication, similarly, the problems in general and in particular are eliminated through medicines called solutions.

Useful tips—acknowledging the truth

- The first truth that needs to be acknowledged is what is true today may not be true tomorrow.
- The second truth is that basic truth never changes; it is the same and constant, only the way it is seen may change.
- Thirdly, one changes with time and either evolves or retreats.
- You will always change till you reach the point of self-realization.
- The truth is your parents love you.
- The truth is that you are not what you think you are.
- The truth is you need to learn more.
- The truth is you need to work harder to know yourself better.
- The truth is once you become successful you would be praised and your reaction to your praises is the real testing time for you.
- The truth is that you are alone but never alone.
- The truth is you will always desire for more.
- The truth is you will get satisfied some day.
- The truth is that there is no truth, yet the truth exists.
- The truth is no one is good or bad, no number is lucky or unlucky but the way you look at it makes it so.
- The truth is that you are successful right now, but another truth is that you don't want to see it.
- The truth which is false today will become true one day and unbelievable shall become believable.

- The truth is we will continue dying and living till we do not reach the ultimate truth.
- The truth is that truth never lies.

Answering the questions given below is not as important as answering these questions with full sincerity. This will help you individuate/ self-realize the ideas and emotions that you carried about life and will help you understand how much of it is valid.

Q1. How do you think you get success in life? What role do you think God /Nature plays in your success?

_____
_____
_____
_____
_____
_____

Q2. Do you think you are popular with the following categories? Give reasons to support your answer?

- FATHER

_____
_____
_____
_____
_____
_____

- MOTHER

_____
_____
_____
_____
_____
_____

• GRAND PARENTS

_____
_____
_____
_____
_____

• TEACHER

_____
_____
_____
_____
_____

• FRIENDS

_____
_____
_____
_____
_____

Q3. Write in two hundred words and give reasons for :—
(A) Person you love most

_____
_____
_____
_____
_____

Person you love to hate and why?
_____
_____
_____
_____
_____
_____

☐☐☐

Chapter 2

Positive Learning

Experience

Once upon a time, a King called his servant and said, 'Come, good fellow, go and gather together in one place all the men born blind... and show them an elephant.' 'Very good, sir,' replied the servant, and he did as he was told. He said to the blind men assembled there, 'Here is an elephant,' and to one man he presented the head of the elephant, to another its ears, to another a tusk, to another the trunk, the foot, back, tail, and tuft of the tail, saying to each one that that was the elephant.

"When the blind men had felt the elephant, the King went to each of them and said to each, 'Well, blind man, have you seen the elephant? Tell me, what sort of thing is an elephant?'

"Thereupon the men who were presented with the head answered, 'Sir, an elephant is like a pot.' And the men who had observed the ear replied, 'An elephant is like a winnowing basket.' Those who had been presented with a tusk said it was a ploughshare. Those who knew only the trunk said it was a plough; others said the body was a grainery; the foot, a pillar; the back, a mortar; the tail, a pestle; the tuft of the tail, a brush.

Then they began to quarrel, shouting, 'Yes it is!' 'No, it is not!' 'An elephant is not that!' 'Yes, it's like that!' and so on, till they came to blows over the matter.

Message

This is what happens to all of us all the time in our lives. We stay convinced that we know more than the other and as everyone thinks the same, no learning happens as everyone is busy in displaying what they already know. If you meet the same people who claim to be the wisest today after two years they would accept that they are wiser than what they were before. And this time also they would say, now I am complete with knowledge. But you know that they are once again talking aimlessly. But with such people learning happens at a slow pace and their learning is also limited to their experience, which happened with their perception. The perception of the other person with same experience may be different. For instance, one may say glass is half empty and the other might say glass is half full. Hence, once again, limited and paradoxical learning takes place in our lives from which we have to beware. Let us understand more with another story.

Experience

A rich farmer once recruited a man who needed a job. The job required the man to cut five trees a day. After the

first day's work, the man realized that he had actually cut six trees, one more than his target of five. He was a happy man. He could not resist the temptation of sharing his achievement. Hence, he presented himself in front of his master and boasted about his achievement. He also promised his master to cut even more trees than what he had done that day.

On the second day, full of enthusiasm and high hopes, he started cutting the trees, but at the end of the day, to his dismay he was only able to cut five trees. He told himself probably it was not his day but certainly the following day he will cut at least seven trees. This did not happen. But what surprised him even more was that he was able to cut only four trees in a day. Each day he saw lesser number of trees coming down and his sincere efforts was not giving him results. Disappointed, he went to his master and narrated to him the whole story. To this, his master asked, "When was the last time you sharpened your axe?"

Message

In this anecdote, you will see that it was not predestined that the man will cut six trees on the first day followed by five in the second and four on the third day. The responsibilities of all the results of all the three days were on the man and nobody else. And this happens with most of us all the time. Instead of finding the problem, we tend to blame it on external factors and hope against hope that someday things will get magically fine. One day, I will score good marks. One day, I will come first in the class. One day, my friends will envy me. Some day, I will get a job. Some day, I will get settled in life with a good salary package. Some day I will become rich and famous and yes we all study, slog and struggle to come to a common objective of becoming rich and famous one day. Hence, there is no learning but a lot of hope.

We all desire to get recognition, bring in laurels to our family members and ourselves, do well in life and be respected by one and all. We all wish to become a known face in the world where people are waiting to meet us, take our autographs. And the desires go on and on.

But strangely enough, not more than 1% people actualize this common desire to do well in life. The result is the rest 99% spend their time blaming God, colleagues, relatives, friends, foes etc.

The moral of the discussion through stories is that working hard is not the only key to success but working smart is equally important. Surely, working smart cannot happen if the learning is either incomplete or does not take place at all. Everything including analysis, success, failure, knowledge etc. are all embodied in the rules of nature. When an individual's life is in harmony with himself, then he is destined to reach his goals in all glory.

There is another misconception we have got to be beware of. We often strongly feel that we know ourselves very well. We tend to think and get convinced invariably that we know exactly how we are going to react in specific situations. But we must also acknowledge the fact that most of the time when specific situations come, we don't react in the way we had thought we would. Hence, we apparently think of knowing our behaviour and habits, but more often than not, our knowing decisively comes out to be untrue about the self. Yes, most of the time we act and behave differently than what we are used to. The reason for behaving differently is that we tend to loose our control and composure, which we had never thought of losing. This once again is invariably due to us not actually knowing ourselves as well as we think we do.

If you have been driving a car for say 5-7 years, you would be confident of taking your car anywhere and driving it with perfection. Also, you would see car accidents happening here and there and probably you would compliment yourself for the mastery you have on the car. But don't be surprised if one day your car also goes out of control. Similarly, when we are under the illusion of knowing ourselves well and think we can control our actions and behaviour. And when we act otherwise, we should accept that we have got to know ourselves better than what we think. We reason it out by saying otherwise, my behaviour would not have been different. Another observation is that when we don't know ourselves well enough, we regret about our behaviours and manner of conduct and blame not ourselves but uncertainties and others instead of comprehending the what's and why's of our lives!!

The reality is, we actually don't know exactly who we are though we think we know ourselves well. That is the reason for going out of control. But there is nothing to feel awkward about, until you accept your behavioural blunders. Through this book, you will not only understand the subtle Laws of Nature and success but you will start knowing yourself better than before. Yes, the scope of improving is one hundred times and who knows, you might just be someone who changes from Mr. Nobody to Mr. Everybody.

Experience

A student went to his master and said to him, " Sir, I want success". The master looked at the young man and did not speak, but smiled. The young man came everyday and insisted on the secrets of success. But he did not get any response from the master except a smile.

One day, when it was very hot, the master asked the young man to go to the river and take a plunge. The young man plunged in and the old man followed him and held the young man down under the water by force. After the young man had struggled for a while, he let him go and asked him what he wanted most while he was under the water. "A breath of air", the disciple answered. "Do you want success in that way? If you do, you will get it right now".

Message

To get success, one has to be prepared to struggle. Also the passion should be so high that one is ready to even sacrifice his life for it. Therefore, one should keep learning about the profession in which he wants to succeed. As already stated, the desire should be so strong that he should be ready to die for the same. Otherwise one can comfortably say that the individual was not serious about the profession but was just pretending to be serious about it.

To know yourself better and to change yourself from nobody to somebody, you will have to keep answering several questions in this book. I am assuming that you have patience, perseverance, and honesty to answer these questions because you are sincerely looking for unbelievable positive transformations in yourself.

Sentence completion Test:

From the phrase, please complete the sentence and give reasons from your sentence/response—Why? How? And When?
　1. I like...............
　2. I hate.............

3. People...............
4. Sex..................
5. My mother..............
6. My father.............
7. I will never......................
8. I want to.......................
9. I love................
10. God...................
11. Sin................
12. I have.........
13. My friends...
14. Friends..........
15. Women................
16. I wish...............
17. I cannot...............

Q1. Why do you think positive learning is essential?

_____
_____
_____
_____
_____
_____

Q2. When you face a problem, do you react immediately or do you think for a while on how to react?

_____
_____
_____
_____
_____
_____

Q3. Identify the thoughts that came into your mind before seeing this question? Describe whether they were positive or negative in nature and what circumstances were prevalent during that time? Did you learn or decide anything from that moment's experience?

_____
_____
_____
_____
_____

Q4. What are the worst experiences you have ever faced in your life? How did you react to them? Do you justify your reactions? If yes, why? And if not, what are the alternative reactions you could have done? If you face the same situation now, how will you react?

_____
_____
_____
_____
_____
_____
_____
_____

Q5. Who is your ideal/hero in life? Why? Give at least three reasons to support it? How did he/she influence your life? What are the things that you have learnt from your ideal person?

_____
_____
_____
_____
_____
_____
_____
_____

Q6. Think about the situations in which you feel insecure and uncomfortable. Pen down your thoughts how you react in those situations and why?

_____
_____
_____
_____
_____
_____
_____
_____

Q7. How do you perceive a problem? Is it helpful in any way for you? Or is it harmful/destructive?

_____
_____
_____
_____
_____
_____
_____
_____

Q8. Are you in the habit of seeing only the negative side of things happening to you? If yes, do you want to continue or do you want to change? If you want to change, how and what steps would you suggest with an appropriate example/situation?

_____
_____
_____
_____
_____
_____
_____

After attempting these exercises sincerely, read the first question and your answer again and contemplate on the written answer. Why did I write this? Am I truly writing what I do and think? Am I trying to evade the fact by ignoring it and hence, not writing it? Am I feeling irritated about not writing something that I know should have been written?

When you ask yourself the above questions they should not be asked just once but at least five times. Read the first question and write down the answer. Read the same question again and write down the answer again. Keep repeating this at least five times. Now compare your answers. If done honestly you would see that the 5th answer would be the most detailed and closest to the answer that you are trying to achieve.

Positive Learning is complicated till one does not practice it to perfection. Once that is done then it gets converted into habit and then it starts controlling you. Positive Learning is more about honesty, integrity, and sincerity. Do everything with these three characteristics. Negative Learning is more about *masala (Newspaper page 3)*. The *masala* that is affecting us in our lives, the *masala* about others and at times enjoying it and at other times crying because of it. We all love *masala* in the food; otherwise we find food tasteless. Similarly, Positive Learning is all about tastelessness but the results that it can bestow upon you cannot be achieved by Negative Learning.

What is Negative Learning?

Negative Learning is about experiencing things that in no way affect our lives positively. Needless to say, we all have aims/objectives/ambitions in our lives. Negative Learning compels us to take the shortest route to this ambition without being sensitive to those who would suffer in the process because of it.

In school, you would have experienced Negative Learning quite often. Try remembering, a student in your class who was weak, who used to sit quietly, was low in confidence. You harassed him and always looked at him with eyes of contempt. Do you think doing this was positive in any way? You did it probably because you enjoyed it. And when you persisted with your wrong doings by insulting your class fellow, it turned into a habit. Obviously, it was negative as there was someone who was not enjoying it though you continued playing your pranks on him.

Hrithik's experience

Hrithik Roshan is a good example of Positive Learning. Hrithik Roshan had a major speech problem. He used to stammer. His father told him to go to U.S.A. and do his M.B.A. and decide there after whether he wanted to work in America or India.

Hrithik told his father that he wanted to work in movies. He went to his office and showed him his portfolio. After much persuasion and convincing his father agreed. This was not the end but the beginning of a struggle for Hrithik. He said, 'I used to keep awake all night, stand in front of the mirror to practice dialogue delivery, when the whole family was fast asleep.' In the morning, he used to go for his Urdu classes followed by his dance classes. He did not have a good body at that point of time and he came to know that Salman Khan was the best person to be consulted about bodybuilding. So, he called Salman Khan and asked for his help. Salman asked him to come to his house. Salman gave him a full schedule about not only the exercises but also about the balanced diet. Now his wife and his then girlfriend Suzzane Khan used to meet Hrithik only in the gym where she used to do all the talking and Hrithik used to do all the exercises. Hrithik in an interview admitted that he did everything what everybody told him including meditation because he never wanted to live with the thoughts that he could have done better had he done something more. He realized that action was in his hands and not the results. He never wanted to live any regret, whether he was a hit or a flop. He wanted to give his best shot without caring about success or failure.

Let us analyze the positive and negative learning through this.

Negative Learning- Let us start with how Hrithik could have negative learning though he was not a negative person. His negative learning could have been "If I have to be a super star, I shall be one. No one can stop me" or " Why do I need to practice dialogue delivery? I can ask for as many cuts as I want, after all, it is my Dad's movie." Or " Enough for the day. I think I should meet my girlfriend. I can practice the rest tomorrow." or "Who needs a good body? Let me just make a good body. Surely a good body is not essential." And the lists and attractions could have gone on with respect to running away from work. But he was a success because he was a man of positive learning.

Message

You would have just got a glimpse of why Positive Learning is so important for success. Like Hrithik, one should do whatever one does wholeheartedly and not just for the sake of doing. One should pull all the humanely possible strings in what one wants to excel, so that he does not regret if he is not successful. One should be convinced that she/he could not have done any better.

Positive Learning is of two types

(a) General Learning *(b) Specific Learning*

General Learning- There is so much of hustle and bustle in a man's life and his environment that he cannot live without observing what is happening in his or someone else's life. He observes new developments taking place in the world and things changing with each passing day. This is more about one's own behavior and other's behavior. He is engrossed in using most of the things available than actually understanding what are the laws that makes it work, e.g., the remote that you so often use to control your television or stereo. Or the electricity that we use or the computer that beautifully functions or the internet etc. No doubt, we get pleasure in using these devices but when it comes to understanding how they function, if you are not an engineer or with scientific bent of mind, you will not enjoy them. General Learning has to do more with survival, being socially acceptable, and learning that may or may not be used in life, largely depending on and creating circumstances. This happens mostly at home and during intervals at schools.

Specific Positive Learning(SPL)- Specific Positive Learning focuses specifically on the profession that will be pursued by an individual for his living. SPL is totally work-oriented in which an individual immerses himself into the subject. The SPL starts right from school. To excel in class, one has to do SPL in studies. An option one has, e.g., X and Y have been given homework by the school. Now X is not inclined towards studies and he goes home and takes his lunch, then sleeps in the afternoon. When he wakes up, he is told by his mother to do the homework, which he promises to do once he is back from playing games. When he gets back, he is instructed by his mother to finish his homework. Suddenly he starts crying, and complains that he is not well. The tantrums that are thrown by X are Specific Negative Learning; whereas Y on the other hand not only finishes his homework but also revises what has been taught in the class. The result is that X just manages to pass whereas Y is in the top five in the class. Now Y could also have thrown many tantrums but he is positive towards his work because he realizes that work given to him should be completed.

In my class, there is another question that I ask: how many times did Thomas Edison fail before making the electric lamp. And the general response is many times. When asked how many times, is it five, seven, hundred, two hundred? People who chose the answer like hundred's etc., my reaction to them is, "It seems you aren't feeling well". Today if people fail few times, they get discouraged and respond that, that career option was not meant for them. They should take up something different. It is because they are not ready to learn from their mistakes. They keep on doing the same thing four to five times and then quit. If you are using the same faulty technique again and again and quit every time, then we will stay where they are. You must learn from your mistakes and try doing things differently. Thomas Edison failed ten thousand times and he never said, "I failed. He said I just learned ten thousand ways in which a thing just won't work." So whatever you want to be in life—Sabeer Bhatia, Edison, Einstein, or Bill Gates—start positive learning from this very moment.

Honesty and integrity are highly essential for Positive Learning. An individual who is not honest will have no scope for positive learning, no matter how much they boast.

We all know the intensity of honesty and the implementation of integrity that we possess. If we say we are unaware of it, it would be another dishonest answer because you have the exact measurement, which either you don't want to explore or share.

Everyone tries to show his best face around as everyone is hungry for praise. But it seems honesty or dishonesty does not matter to the people or the society in general. Hence, one thinks of prospering without it. We may give ourselves hundreds of reasons to be dishonest but one thing is for sure, one can never get to two S's, i.e., Success and satisfaction, without honesty.

This story will show you how do we all think and learn.

King's experience

In a kingdom, there were hundreds of courtiers and each one claimed to be the most loyal and honest to the king and the kingdom. And the king was very proud of each one of them. Often he used to boast about the honesty and sincerity of his courtiers. One day, while he was speaking highly about them, a gentleman came and challenged the king to prove it. To this, the king said that each one of his men were ready to sacrifice their lives for the king at one order.

The gentleman said that he was not interested in asking the king to sacrifice a few people to prove his point because what he was going to ask the king will not only prove the integrity of his men, but also whether they are actually ready to give their lives away.

Channelizing Self for Success

The gentleman asked the courtiers to get milk at night and fill it in a drum, which was kept outside the palace. In the night, all the courtiers came without anyone being absent and filled the drum. But in the morning the drum was found full of water. The courtiers were questioned about what had happened. Each one of them had thought there would be so much milk that the water he was filling in the drum would not be detected.

Message

Somehow, due to an integrity crisis, we all hope someone else will be honest and in the process we excuse ourselves from being honest though we shamelessly boast about our honesty.

Osho's experience

This is the most profound example of Positive Learning. Through this, Osho got self-enlightenment and he came to know about the essence of knowledge, which is still unknown to the majority of the world in spite of various unbelievable advancements.

On March 21, 1953, Osho became enlightened. Here's an abridged version by the great master himself about what he felt prior to that great day and what he experienced.

Osho: I am reminded of the fateful day of March 21, 1953. For many lives, I had been working - working upon myself, struggling, doing whatsoever can be done, and nothing was happening.

Just seven days before March 21, 1953, I stopped working on myself. A moment comes when you see the futility of effort. You have done all that you can do and nothing is happening. You have done all that is humanly possible. Then what else can you do? In sheer helplessness, one drops all search.

And the day the search stopped, the day I was not seeking something, the day I was not expecting something to happen, it started happening. A new energy arose out of nowhere. It was not coming from any source. It was coming from nowhere and everywhere. It was in the trees and in the rocks and the sky and the sun and the air - it was everywhere. And I had been seeking so hard, and I was thinking it is far away. But it was so near and so close.

Just because I was seeking, I had become incapable of seeing what was near. Seeking is always for the far, seeking is always for the distant and thus was not distant. I had become far-sighted, I had lost near-sightedness. The eyes had become focussed on the far away, the horizon, and they had lost the quality to see what is close, surrounding you.

The day effort ceased, I also ceased. Because you cannot exist without effort, or desire or striving.

The day I stopped seeking... and it is not right to say that I stopped seeking. It is better to say, the day seeking stopped. Let me repeat it: the better way to say it is, the day the seeking stopped. Because if I stop it then I am there again. Now stopping becomes my effort, my desire, and desire goes on existing in a very subtle way.

Message

You cannot stop desire; you can only understand it. In the very understanding is the stopping of it. Remember, nobody can stop desiring, and the reality happens only when desire stops. Till then you keep learning to desire and desire to learn.

Chapter 3

Thoughts

Experience of a cub

This is a story of a lioness that died accidentally while hunting for her cub. The cub was looked after by the sheep and he grew with them, ate grass and talked like sheep. After a few years, he was a full grown lion but he always thought like a sheep as he was convinced in his thoughts

that he was a sheep. One day, another lion came in search of prey and was surprised to see a lion in the flock of sheep, fleeing like the sheep at the approach of danger.

He attempted to get near the fleeing lion, trying to tell him that he could not be his prey because he was another lion like him, strong and powerful. But this lion thought himself to be weak in spite of having all the characteristics of a ferocious lion. And one day, this lion caught the fleeing lion and asked him, why he was running away. The fleeing lion exclaimed that since he was a sheep, he would be killed. The lion told him that he was also a lion and took him near a lake and said, "Look here, here is my reflection and yours and none of us look like sheep." And that very minute, the thought of being a sheep disappeared and the fleeing lion also started roaring.

Message

So it was a thought that made a lion a sheep and a thought that made him a lion again. Hence, we should realize the importance of thoughts in our lives. These thoughts control our behaviour and compel us to behave either assertively or aggressively.

Has it ever happened with you that when you are sitting for an exam or appearing for an interview that your thoughts came true? If your thoughts told you that you will not pass in the exam or in the interview even before seeing the question paper or meeting the interviewer, and the result was exactly as you had thought. Looking at the brighter side, it must have also happened with you that before scoring a single goal or a run you knew your team would win and it so happened. If these things have been experienced by you, then there is no other proof than your personal experience to convince you, the importance of thoughts.

Where do our actions come from? Surely, first we think then we act. Thoughts are as potent a tool as actions are. Everything starts from thoughts. First you think then you act. Today, science along with your personal experiences, has enough proof to substantiate that your thoughts make or break you and either you control your thoughts or they will control you.

The mind is the source of all thoughts. Thoughts are then implemented into actions and actions get you corresponding results. Therefore, one should work on the mind with sincerity and not let it loose like a wild elephant. If you do not tame your mind by controlling it, you will not be able to accomplish your desires, because the root of success and failure is determined by the mind.

The mind is the key that opens the door of success or failure in our lives. You might ponder that if the mind is the key to success or failure then why is it that most people open that key towards failure and not success? And the answer is simple. People are either ignorant about the fact that the mind plays a pivotal role in their lives or do not appreciate the power of the mind and hence, take it lightly, or are unconsciously habitual of inviting negative thoughts all the time.

For centuries, the brain has been considered merely as a three and a half pound lump of grey matter. With the invention of the microscope, it was found that the brain is composed of millions of tiny cells called neurons. Then the scientist discovered that each brain cell was like a tiny octopus, having a centre or nucleus and a large number of little tentacles radiating in all directions from it. Each of these tentacles had thousands of tiny protuberances, much like the section pads on the octopus, but protruding from all sides of the tentacles.

The mind being part of brain, has unimaginable capacity. An average man as we know him to be, does not use more than 3% of his mind. The following figures will give you some idea about the capacity of the brain. A brain has a staggering number of individual neurons: 10,000,000,000. The number of pathways and connections that could be made by normal brain cells is 10 million kilometers. Further more it has been calculated that the entire network of the telephone systems of the world, if compared to your brain, would occupy a part of it equal to the size of an ordinary garden pea. It has also been suggested that at any given movement, there are between 1,00,000 and 10,00,000 chemical reactions taking place in your brain.

If these figures are not adequate enough to surprise you, then watch out for the comparison between the human brain and the world's most powerful computer. The super computer, even when working 400 million calculations per second, would, operating for one hundred years, only accomplish what your brain can accomplish in a minute.

And surely there are still many more amazing figures to surprise you and make you realize the importance of thought, rather positive thinking for success. I will also like to point out that what nature is slowly unfolding to our atheist and so called innovative and dynamic scientist has been already said by Lord Krishna five thousand years ago. Lord Krishna has spoken at length about the mind but unfortunately, we do not believe in things unless and until they are scientifically proven. It is because we do not trust in the power of our thoughts. We tend to ignore our creative thoughts and wish to stick to those things that have been told to us scientifically even though our creative thoughts would disagree with them.

The theory of relativity would not have come into existence if Einstein had not followed his thoughts and observation, which was very different from what his formal training said. He discovered his theory of relativity while lying on a hill one summer day not seated in front of his desk. His imagination took him to a place where his formal training in physics told him he should not be. Concerned about this, he went back to his blackboard, and believing his imagination to be more correct than his formal training, worked out new mathematics to explain the truth of what his mind had told him.

Experience of Henry Ford

Henry Ford, the son of a peasant, would not have turned into an industrialist, if he had believed what was the common knowledge of that time. He was always inclined towards the machine: He dared to dream. When he was 12 years old he saw engine car in his village. The next minute, Henry was out of his carriage and talking with the driver. His father insisted that he leave school at the age of 12 as he saw in no way studies could help his son in farming. But Henry's interest in engine was so high that he gained knowledge by studing every scientific magazine he could get his hands on, to know more about their working, and not through formal education. He used to work out in the farm the whole day and on machines till late at night.

The common knowledge in his field was that petrol would never replace steam to make the engine run. But Ford thought otherwise. He kept on working on it while the whole mechanic world criticized him and told him he was a fool. A car could never run on petrol. Suppose you meet 15 people and all of them tell you that you are mad, after a certain point you will too start feeling that there is something wrong with you. But here was Ford, with his thought that the cars could run on petrol and it took 17 long years to prove what he said. Being a brilliant mechanic, he received very lucrative job offers with the conditions that he will have to stop working on petrol engine as it was a useless endeavor. But this man never scummed to these lucrative job offers and carried on doing what he had thought of. It took him 17 long years and countless sacrifices before he finally achieved his goal.

Message

Thanks to people like Einstein and Ford, science and technology respectively have made a big leap. These were the people who listened to their mind, to totally different points of view and their faith could never be shaken by the world.

So, it should be your endeavor to sow those thoughts that reap for you and not against you in life. Needless to say, it is not easy but answering these queries will help you to breed the right kinds of thoughts.

Hence, we have got to think about the thoughts that make us and not break us. But before going on, let us analyze and realize what kind of thoughts you are accustomed to by answering the questions sincerely.

Identify the thoughts that come into your mind two hours before seeing this question? Describe them, whether they were positive or negative in nature and what circumstances were prevalent during that time? What did you learn from them?

_____
_____
_____
_____
_____
_____

Identify the thoughts that keep entering your mind most of the time? Why do you think these particular thoughts always come to your mind?

_____
_____
_____
_____
_____
_____

1. Count the positive thoughts or explanations that you have written. Similarly count the negative thoughts or explanations written by you.

_____
_____
_____
_____
_____
_____

2. Analyze the circumstances that made you think what you thought. Were those circumstances so positive or negative that you thought accordingly or you actually did look at the positive circumstances negatively or negative circumstances positively ?

___

3. Think about the most positive and the negative people in the world that you know. Do you think they would react as you do?

___

4. Now think about Mahatma Gandhi, Sardar Ballabh bhai Patel, Subhas Chandra Bose and how do you think each one of them would have reacted ?

___

5. Now think about people like Charles Sobhraj, Amrish Puri, Amjad Khan (their character in movies) and how would they have reacted?

___

GAINING CONFIDENCE

Experience of the Army with the General

Once upon a time, there was a general who was leading his army into battle against an enemy ten times the size of his own.

Along the way to the battle field, the troops stopped by a small temple to pray for victory.

The general held up a coin and told his troops, "I am going to implore the gods to help us crush our enemy. If this coin lands with the heads on top, we'll win. If its tails, we'll lose. Our fate is in the hands of the Gods. Let's pray wholeheartedly."

After a short prayer, the general tossed the coin. It landed

with the heads on top. The troops were overjoyed and went into the battle with high spirits.

Just as predicted, the smaller army won the battle.

The soldiers were elated, "It's good to have the gods on our side! No one can change what they have determined."

"Really?" The general showed them the coin— on both sides were heads.

Message

Nothing is impossible in this world. If we believe anything to be impossible for us, we are only reinforcing the conviction that we shall not be able to perform the task. But if we see someone else performing the same task, then we can never exclaim that it is not possible. It is all in our mind and we have got to help our mind become either our friend or foe.

What should I do? How do I do it? These two questions are enough to show that the confidence level of an individual, if not low, is questionable. Such small thoughts haunt us right from the childhood but have their maximum impact after we have appeared for our class X exams. This phase is supposed to be important because we start giving shape to our career by choosing a particular stream. The next phase is when we get our class XII results. We tend to visit counselors and educationists seeking their assistance on choosing the right career. But more often than not, we tend to understand that the answer is lying within us and not outside us.

Most of the time we tend to ignore our sixth sense or imagination, as we believe that it is unscientific and baseless. Moreover, we get vexed when such thoughts come back to us, as we don't want to make ourselves look stupid and irrational in this modern world. Hence, we close the doors of thoughts and attempt to think rationally the way the world/ an intelligent human being should think. We don't realize that by being compliant to the world, we are loosing our originality and creativity just because the world does not accept our new phenomenally creative theory. In other words, if the world is undynamic, so you should be. One should accept the fact that the world has never been open to change and it will always initially resist to it. Only one thing in this world is permanent and that is change. One tends to forget this very often. And all this leads to low self-esteem or confidence.

One does not realize that by nurturing the creative thoughts, defending and protecting them and applying them in one's life gives us tremendous confidence. We keep talking about self-confidence but one should ask himself if one is seriously looking to increase self-confidence or one is just crying and complaining about it to gain sympathy. If it is the former then the second question one should ask himself is, 'What am I doing to increase my confidence level ?' One expects things should happen magically with him, i.e., one day he gets up and finds himself full of confidence, but, unfortunately that only happens in dreams.

How can I increase my confidence level?

To increase self-confidence, you will have to be true to yourself and your ideas by thinking over your ideas and thoughts deeply and not ignoring them. It does not matter where they come from, i.e., through experience, observation, sixth sense etc. You should have the courage to tell the world how you think. And if you don't agree, please tell me where and why I am wrong with a condition that your disagreement should be based on logic. You should not succumb to the pressure of the world to give up your thoughts and ideas. It should not be so that if 50 people are on one side and instead of proving you wrong they are shouting and pressurizing you to give up your thought. Do you think you should be doing that ? If Henry Ford would have done the same by coming under pressure from the world that cars cannot run on petrol, then certainly we would not have cars running on petrol. If you are made to give up your thoughts, how would you feel ? Your self-esteem will certainly go down because you surrendered to the number that was against you and not logic. What will you tell yourself ? You will fall in your own eyes, no matter how much artificial make-up you wear and try to fool the world. You cannot fool yourself since you were low on confidence and risk taking ability, you failed.

Magical Tips

Tell yourself that you have the capacity to achieve your definite goal in life and you will try persistently for it till you succeed. And that here and now you promise such action. Imagine yourself doing what you have always wanted to do in your life for 15 minutes everyday. For the first 2-3 days, nothing will happen to your imagination. Then suddenly you will start seeing high self-esteem and start getting ideas that you had never imagined or thought about, e.g, if you see yourself as a successful sales executive then imagine wearing a formal white/pink/blue shirt with a formal trouser and a tie. Then see yourself shaking hands with a customer while introducing the product. See the smile on your face. See yourself handling questions put across by the customer in an efficient, easy manner. See yourself collecting the order and driving back to your office. Similarly, see yourself handling different types of customers, their reactions and your actions.

The reason for a low confidence level at times is also when others hurt us and we are not able to respond either due to fear that he will get hurt if you reciprocate in the similar way. Or at times we have the fear of parting away with that person and we realize that we are heavily dependent on him. Therefore, we will not say anything to him that we are dying to say. Also, at times we get stunned when we are told something and it is only after we reach home, we start realizing that there were so many ways in which we could have reacted. When facing such problems, go to your room, sit with crossed legs and imagine the situation. Then start looking for the answers about how you could have reacted. The answer would be in several options to the person realize that he was wrong. Obviously, the solutions cannot help you now but can prepare you for the near future, as you now know exactly how you should react. Normally, we do not do this. If some one insults us, we quietly take the insult, abuse that person within ourselves or pity ourselves and then forget about the situation. We do not realize that whenever that situation comes back at us we are always vulnerable to it. It is not that we are too good a person but it is because we react out of helplessness and we have never prepared ourselves from the experiences.

Must follow tips

SAY TO YOURSELF THE FOLLOWING

I have full faith in God and his laws. Therefore, I will follow his laws with full dedication and determination and will never ever quit no matter how difficult circumstances may be and I know that I have the power to do this.

To be successful, I have to see everyone with equality, as God has made everyone and is in everybody. If I disrespect others, I will be disrespecting God. I will treat the rich and the poor, relatives and strangers, friends and enemies equally and I know I have the power to do this.

I will make at least five friends in a month and that too with my own initiative and I know I have the power to do this.

I will inculcate love for mankind in myself and will eliminate selfishness, jealousy, hatred, envy and I know I have the power to do this.

I will pray for fifteen minutes everyday. Praying to God with full concentration and also talking and seeking his guidance or how I should do away with my difficulties. I will also imagine myself doing what I want to do in the future and I know I have the power to do this.

I also know that I have to train my subconscious mind with positive thoughts. Therefore, I will feed my mind with positive thoughts and will not do any wrong, and I know I have the power to do this.

❏❏❏

Chapter 4

Meditation

Experience of a blind frog

Once upon a time, there was a frog's race .The goal was to reach the top of a high tower. Many people gathered to see and support them. The race began. In reality, the people didn't believe that it was possible for the frogs to reach the top of the tower, and all the negative phrases that one could think of, were shouted at the frogs.

"What pain!!! They'll never make it!"

The frogs began to resign, except for one who kept on climbing and the people continued to instigate it.

At the end, all the frogs quit, except the one who, alone and with enormous efforts, reached the top of the tower.

The others wanted to know how did he do it. One of the frogs approached him to ask how he had finished the race.

And discovered that he... was deaf!

Never listen to people who have the bad habit of being negative...

Message

The deaf frog meditated on his aim and where he wanted to be. He went ahead with what he had to do and so his concentration and focus level went along with him. He did not leave anything positive behind except discouragement and negativitism and this enabled him to win the race.

When one meditates, apart from outside discouragement that generally comes in from the people who have never tried meditation, there are others who have attended a few classes just to gain some knowledge about it and criticize by exclaiming that it does not work. But it works for people who are deaf to the outside world and who follow it sincerely, and know the results. Meditation is something that has to be felt and not talked about.

If you want genuine peace, happiness, prosperity, and satisfaction, meditation is one of the most powerful tools, which will get you all these and that too in no time. Meditation can bring you whatever you were craving for; it can also get rid of your cravings; it can show you a new door towards life; and above all it is not only knowledge but also the key to the implementation of that knowledge. It does not take you away from your goal but it gives you strength to pursue it more effectively. It gives you clarity of thoughts; it helps you to concentrate and makes your life full of quality living.

But if you think that meditation can immediately relieve you of your stress and bring you immediate happiness and joy, then I am afraid you are expecting too much from this powerful tool. Yes, it is powerful in the long run but your expectations should be realistic. Magic happens only in fantasies.

How did meditation start?

It all started thousands of years ago when the great sages were immersed in, trying to answer queries such as who are we and why are we here. What are we supposed to achieve? What is Death? Is there any life after death? From where did we come? Where shall we go?

These and many more queries, they tried finding in their environment, on this great planet earth. Generations after generations, they kept trying to find out the true meaning of life and they were disappointed. Their curiosity was so intense that they wanted to know the unknown and its source and were not interested in knowing anything less.

As the time went by disappointed, they contemplated on seeing what was inside them, what they were made of. This was the time when they closed their eyes and started trying to find out the source of their origin, which they eventually did. But the ecstasy, bliss, and joy was only for them and they were unable to explain it to the others and because of this, others found it difficult to believe them. Yet they were neither lamented or called pretenders. This was because the locals would come to these sages with their problems, which the sages were able to solve. Hence, people believed that these sages had some unknown power. But what it was and how they got it was a mystery for them. Surely, they were not qualified to understand it.

So, meditation has been a magical thought of controlling and regulating the mind and body on which our success depends. Meditation is one of the paths to realization and if done sincerely, it unfolds inexplicable experiences within you. To put it simply, meditation is highly relaxing, joyful, and destressing exercise that also gives you opportunity to know the unknown. The results of it are also immediate in the sense that an individual starts feeling free from stress almost immediately–during or after the meditation. But the purpose of meditation should not be selfish otherwise I don't see any meaning attached to it spiritually. It should not be carried out only to come out of work pressure etc. to an extent. Meditation is primairly of two types.

Must follow tips

But before getting into the two types of meditation let us keep the following things in mind.
- You should find a clean, peaceful room for meditation.
- Make sure that you have done whatever you were required to do, so that there is no interference in the form of phone calls or visitors coming in. That is the reason that the best time considered for meditation is either midnight or early morning when the commotion is at its minimal and when an individual can be with himself. However, there is no auspicious or inauspicious time for meditation.
- Also meditation should not be done because you have to do it, as it will not be meditation but fooling yourself.
- Also if you don't feel like meditating and it has been happening for a couple of days, then start with reading good spiritual books or the Bhagvad Gita. It will help you get back to the said mode.
- Don't lament if you are unable to meditate well.
- Don't lament if your meditation was shorter than the time you generally sit for it.
- Don't take out any reasons for not doing it properly.
- Don't compare your meditation today with the previous day.
- Don't think about time while meditating.
- Let yourself loose and don't bother about whether you are following the right steps or not. Your intention, intensity and sincerity is necessary and nothing more or less.

How does this short term (Type - I) meditation work?

There are no short cuts in life and hence, there is no

meditation technique that would make you achieve what others might achieve in more time. People who claim this are wrong because God being above all this, is certainly not concerned under which guru you are training or which posture you are sitting in and hence, would be rewarded accordingly. God only observes with what intention you are doing it and how much reward should be given to you. Remember, the reward would be in proportion of the effort you make, not even 1 decimal here or there.

In this short cut meditation, you are supposed to concentrate on a mantra, a word and you are supposed to focus on it. You keep saying it over and over again till the time you get lost in it .So the mantra here is not the destination, but a medium to the destination called stress reliever or buster or *shoonya*. When you want to come out of it, you do it by chanting this mantra in your mind slowly. This mantra as already suggested, is the vehicle that takes you to temporary peace, but once you are out of it, the effect might last 2-3 hours. Thereafter, you are the same old being with nothing much spiritual happening to you. In this, one does not have any urge to know the unknown, but one meditating his need and selfish interests.

Why I call it a short cut meditation is because one is only focusing on his needs and desires and there is no evolution in the individual's growth in the long run. But yes, the short cut meditation can also take you to longer meditation if you enjoy meditating. If you want to know the source from which you have been getting the bliss, joy, and satisfaction, then long term meditation is the key.

The long term (Type - II) meditation

Now, coming to the real world of meditation in which the individual and also the techniques are not for immediate benefit but for the long run. Yes, the benefits in this meditation will be everlasting and the meditator does this not for himself/ herself but to go to his true home where he will get everlasting knowledge, success, and satisfaction and where he will not have to lose one thing to get another one. He will be God like with no longings and desires.

The reasons for calling it a long-term meditation is because various names have been given to the meditation by various gurus preaching it. However, the source, method and objective remains the same. Whether you call it *kriya yoga* or *sudarshan kriya* or any other *kriya*, it is and will remain a pure long-term meditation for me.

I know this is not a spiritual book but life cannot go on without progressing and learning. Hence, in long-term meditation or the real meditation as Vinod Khanna, the famous actor said, " Normally people think meditation calms you down. But it can actually make you go through all kinds of experiences. It can frighten you, agitate you, and irritate you. You might want to run away from it."

Yes, this is a bit startling but this is also true. Imagine meditation giving you stress when you have come for a stress buster. In fact, it is not the meditation doing it but through meditation your mind is getting cleared and this clearing process is trying to suggest that more burden is being put on you, which is untrue. If you are trying to put the fire off, what happens when you attempt to do so ? Yes, it aggravates further for sometime and then finally comes under control. Similarly, through meditation your mind and habits are getting agitated and are trying to scare you from it. But if you persist for some time, then there is no reason that stress, anxiety, fear, pressure will not disappear and you will be a changed man who will keep progressing in life, both spiritually as well as materialistically.

Golden tips

The right way for doing meditation
- Please bear in mind the points already stated above.
- There is no strict posture. One can either meditate on the floor or on the bed or chair. But the place should be clean and as noiseless as possible.
- Try keeping your back/ spine straight. Try not to support it with the back of your chair or the bed or anything else. Initially, you may not be able to sit

with the straight spine as you are not used to it, but try to sit straight for a longer period of time.
- If you are not able to keep the spine straight there is no problem with that. Sit as comfortably as you can.
- After sitting, comfortably relax your body. Just relax and close your eyes.
- Just keep sitting in a relaxed manner with eyes closed. Thoughts will start pouring in your mind but ignore them. Keep observing your thoughts for they will come and go. Don't penetrate into your thoughts otherwise they will sway you to some other side of story. (You can also play some cassettes like OM by Pandit Jasraj, as it will be a help to you to concentrate initially but this should not be made into a habit, you are competent to meditate without any external help after sometime).
- Now with closed eyes concentrate on the point between the eyebrows. Don't force yourself to concentrate in-between the eyebrows otherwise you will get a headache. Obviously, we are not doing this for headache.
- Now breathe in, retain and then breathe out. (If you are breathing in say for 5 seconds, retain your breath for another five seconds and then release it in five seconds.) Remember your breathing in and out pattern should not fluctuate i.e. Taking breath in 5 seconds. Retaining in for 6 and exhaling in 7 seconds. Do it for 4-5 minutes or till the time you are comfortable with it or you enjoy doing it.
- Now concentrate on the bottom part of your spine and when you inhale see your breath travelling from the bottom up your spine and when you exhale see your breath going from the top to the bottom of your spine and keep chanting in your mind *om, om, om, om...* (Keep doing it till you enjoy and don't exert yourself).
- Next, enjoy the time of breathlessness when you are neither inhaling nor exhaling. You would see a time when after taking and releasing the breath, your body is motionless and does not want to breathe for a few seconds (From two seconds to — depending upon the individual).

- At the end, close both your ears and you will suddenly hear a sound. Just concentrate on that sound and keep chanting *om, om, om*...(You may get tired quickly because your hands will have no place to rest when they are on your ears. So take some pillows or have a table to rest your arms on while meditating)

As I have been mentioning again and again, this meditation is a powerful tool if done with full sincerity. While meditating, you can visualize any God/ Goddess that you believe in. Also, show your sincerity to God that you want to know Him and be with Him by surrendering everything to Him. Tell Him "I am your child, you are my father and my mother and I don't want anything in life besides you". If your commitment towards him is the fullest then you will certainly find Him without fail. But if it is that O God I am meditating so that I get peace, prosperity etc., then there is no point in fooling yourself because you can attract purity only if you are clean and pure in your intention and thoughts.

God bestows everything on his children who are sincere towards Him. He has let no one down and will never do so. One should have clean karmas and remember to be assertive.

Life is not as complicated as it is seen or shown. Similarly, meditation is not as complicated as it is depicted. After all, God does not want us to do difficult things but He can be easily known, if we do simple and straight things right.

Given below are questions which will help you to be in the track with what, how, and when you are doing your meditation. These exercises will force you to come with answers and solutions to the questions and problems, respectively. It will also help you to measure how life is turning and changing with you and for you.

> How was your first day of meditation ? Write down your experience?
>
> _____
>
> _____

_____
_____
_____

How was your first week of meditation? Explain.
_____
_____
_____
_____
_____

How was your second week of meditation?
_____
_____
_____
_____
_____

How was your first month of meditation?
_____
_____
_____
_____
_____

How was your second month of meditation?
_____
_____
_____
_____
_____

Concentration, focus and solace

A man excels who is able to concentrate on concentration.

There is a difference between concentration and focus. Concentration is used to concentrate or fix your mind on anything in general. For example, I am not able to concentrate in studies. You might be focused towards studies, yet you may not be able to concentrate on it.

To focus means to put all the effort and energy of your mind towards something specific; it could be studies, work, assignments , games etc. It means you are ready or prepared to do anything for it and you are thinking about it most of the time. You want to excel in that particular thing and as far as your immediate objective or goal is concerned, yes, it has been streamlined by you. You would like to, if given a chance, to create an opportunity to excel in it. Concentration is implementation of all that has been just mentioned.

It is concentration that gives us solace, peace and satisfaction. It is solace that gives us concentration. If we are unable to concentrate, we get restless, we feel guilty, and hopeless. Inspite of wanting and trying to concentrate we are unable to do it.

We should ask ourselves : Do we actually want to concentrate or hope to concentrate? If we are hoping to concentrate, then we are leaving the onus on some outside force, which will enable us to concentrate. In the first chapter, we have already seen, that we are responsible for ourselves. If we are unable to concentrate, we should blame ourselves for not being able to concentrate.

A child used to complain to his father often of not being able to concentrate in his studies. One day, the child's father brought him a cricket kit and told him to play with his friends. After five hours, the father told his son to come back home but the child replied that he wanted to play some more. Eventually, when the kid was back home, the father asked him, "In spite of having a low concentration level, how were you able to concentrate on the cricket field for six hours?"

The son replied, "I never knew how the time flew".

This is what happens with most of us. We have always taken games as a source of enjoyment. Studies and work in the office on the other hand are supposed to be the source of tension and responsibility. The problem is not with the object, that we are unable to concentrate. The problem is in our perception about that object, that it is hard, difficult, too challenging or not worth to invest so much of our resources in it.

Needless to say, concentration is the key to success. Today, man is fighting hard with himself to concentrate as he realizes the importance of it. Paradoxically, as he is fighting to concentrate, it is the reason that he is not able to concentrate on anything. He focuses on a thing because he thinks that he has to morally do so, his counterparts are doing it, society is demanding it from him and if he is unable to come up to the expectations of others, it will be considered immoral. This guilt and fear of not being able to concentrate destroys his concentration towards the goal and he unconsciously concentrates on guilt and fear, thereby losing his focus.

We all have equal power of concentration. At least our minds are equally powerful. You would be surprised to know that we all are concentrating all the time, the only difference is that some people are concentrating on a purpose and some are concentrating on the fears that have been bothering us for a long time. There are others who concentrate on how to make one's action destructive.

Why am I not being able to concentrate?

There may be a myriad of reasons why you are not able to focus or concentrate on the job at hand. As I stated earlier, we always concentrate all the time. Even when we think we are not able to concentrate at a point of time, then too we are focusing on something. What is that something? It is something else. So let us find out, what is that something else we invariably focus on.

You are probably doing something you don't enjoy. When we keep thinking in our head and are occasionally voracious at home about the work we dislike doing. Hence, we keep telling ourselves, "I don't like this job". Yet we do it for our livelihood. This has been seen particularly in people who give up their life-long ambitions which they have been obsessed with, or with which they had high hopes and expectations and which was their first love. Eventually, the majority of people give up their ambitions for a safer and happier life, which gives them security to an extent but takes away their satisfaction for ever.

So, when we don't enjoy doing something, it is about getting disinterested in it. This happens or must have happened in school when we liked a few subjects and disliked others. Some students are fond of science, while others are fond of arts. Till class X, when an art lover has to study science, he curses physics, chemistry, and mathematics and hopes he will finish with them sooner than later. He concentrates more on hating the subject, rather than understanding its essence and utility.

The next stage is college and more often than not, students like choosing colleges over the courses. Even today, every student dreams of going to the north campus in Delhi, and is ready to compromise with his subject or the area of interest., e.g., a student is interested in pursuing B.Com (H) but he is not getting admission in specific elite colleges or where his clan of school friends have taken admission in. Hence, he takes B.A. (P). He is not interested in this stream but he does not want to leave his friend or go away from a dream college. So, he will not be able to concentrate on B. A. (P) and will find it boring. Here he has concentrated on a good college or being with friends rather than concentrating on the subject. The focus was there but the area of focus ended when he got the admission in B.A. (P). Thus, the area of focus was short-lived. If he had taken B.Com (H), the area of focus would have been long lived.

Next step is job/ employment and by this time the majority of the people have left their ambitions and the area of focus. They start with a particular job. Not more than 20 % succeed in getting what they want and the rest 80 % start focusing from a particular job to any job. This is where the concentration or the focus level takes a fall. The individual thinks he has been imposed upon with this job because of society and circumstances and hence, he has to live with it. He dreads to dream again and focuses till the point where he is not kicked out of the job.

Lack of knowledge- When we have a job in hand about which we have incomplete knowledge, we cannot concentrate. Instead, we concentrate on not having that full knowledge, which makes us feel miserable. The reason for incomplete knowledge could be lack of it or our incapacity to gather it. Why do you think tuition centres are mushrooming everywhere? The reason is, today, schools and teachers are not being able to provide adequate knowledge to the students. Teachers themselves are low on knowledge, specially in small towns. The main reason for this is that today schools focus on finishing their courseware rather than trying to know if students are really learning what they are taught. This is ensured by tuition centres. Also, the other factor is that students are not focusing on their studies as they like focusing on games, drama, arts etc. This situation is similar to the first case that we have discussed.

The same rules apply in our next stage of life i.e: work. We either don't possess knowledge and probably we tend to lie during the interview and put ourselves in a fix. So we start concentrating on what will be the reaction of the office or how can I ensure that the office does not know about it. The reason for incomplete knowledge can also be the lack of training or the lack of quality training provided by the office, or the bad attitude and communication skills of the boss, which prevents an individual from learning.

Lack of skills

Today, Emotional Quotient has become as popular as Intelligence Quotient. IQ deals with knowledge, but EQ deals with how effectively you transmit and communicate that knowledge. The importance of a good EQ of managing one's emotions skillfully is so important, that is why the corporate world go to management and engineering colleges for recruitment, to appoint people with high IQ. At the same time they, don't want to compromise on the EQ. Hence, if they find a boy with 90% IQ but is introvert and does not believe in sharing. They prefer taking a student with IQ of 70 % but who is an extrovert, is popular with friends, and is a team player. Showing knowledge is more important than having it but not showing.

If we don't have appropriate emotional quotient skills, people tend to become less interested in us, when that happens we are not able to focus and our concentration level goes down. Instead of focusing on our behaviour, we start focusing on other people's behaviour and the result is we get irritated, become bitchy, jealous, negative etc.

Lack of determination

It may be also that you are projecting yourself to be very serious about things but actually you are not. You are not only fooling yourself but others too. As a result, you not only feel guilty but are in no position to concentrate, as you actually don't want to do so. High determination level takes an individual a long way into concentration but if one does not have any aim/ goal in what he is doing, it is a sheer waste of time and whatever little effort he has put in. In fact, it is much tougher to sit and pretend than try and find out the right way of doing something even though you may not find it interesting.

Useful tips
- Don't dream and hope. Rather, work on the problem.
- Replace laziness with being proactive and build up stamina.
- Contemplate within the work.
- Destress from time to time with what you want to do.
- Throw negative attitudes out of your system.
- Don't fear anything.
- Be patient.
- Don't compare too often.

1. *Self-introspection exercise-*

When you do or try to do a particular activity just write down on a sheet of paper what comes into your mind that prevents you from doing it well (from inside-personal and outside-environment). Just for 10 minutes think how, where, why - (instinct, habit, obsession). Until and unless you solved/ minimized the external/internal disturbances, decide/punish yourself that you will not do the activity. Try to assess the internal body needs at that very moment, and go deep into your body and those parts which are going to be involved in a particular activity. At the same time, be totally aware of the momentary situational demands and condition. Encourage your identified body parts that you are going

Channelizing Self for Success

to do it and that you cannot escape! It's your responsibility! Do it now.

2. Meditation/focus attention on a particular object like a candle, mirror, etc.

Good concentration leads to good focus in life towards your goals. Life is all about ups and downs. It makes us look like a king at times and at other times like a fool, worthless, and probably a slave. We like our profession at one time and we feel that we should be with it for ever because we understand it so well. Since, we have complete control over it and will not only make us successful but popular as well.

Experience of De witt Wallace

This is an example of this great man who remained focused towards his job with sincerity throughout; so much so that he not only got money but was a true self-made man. This also got him world-wide respect. Once, he landed in the city hospital with a broken leg. The leg was plastered and he had to be in the hospital for quite some time. He had time but nothing to do, so he started reading all the magazines he could lay his hands on. When he was through with all of them and did not know what to do, he went through the interesting pages of the magazines again and edited them in fewer words. By the time he was discharged from the hospital he had edited quite a few number of articles. He then thought of sending, his manuscript to all the publishers in U.S.A asking them to start a magazine by making him the editor.

He expected a big response but to his disappointment he received just two letters : one from a publisher who wanted to print it but was not interested in making Wallace the editor ; and the other publisher was so big that he thought it was too small an offer for him. Hence, he also withdrew.

This man went on editing and came up with his own magazine. For this, he had to borrow money. But he did not have money for the second edition. However, he did not lose his focus. He worked as a librarian, used his free time to write condensed articles, since he could not afford to buy books. But he did not lose his focus. He stayed in a rented house, which he further had to sublet because he needed money. But he did not lose his focus. He did not lose his focus amidst his difficulties and that is the reason you are able to read a beautiful magazine called 'Readers Digest,' not to mention millions and millions of dollars De witt Wallace earned.

Message

Don't lose focus. Otherwise, along with it you will also lose concentration. If you start losing one thing, you automatically start losing the rest as well. Keep this in mind and meditate, focus and concentrate joyfully but not forcefully.

Chapter 5

Forgiveness

Experiences of two different men

One day, a famous government officer met a highly respected elderly master. Being conceited, he wanted to prove that he was a superior person.

As their conversation carried on, he asked the master, "Old man, do you know what I think of you and the things you say?"

The master replied, "I don't care what you think of me. You are entitled to have your own opinion."

The officer snorted, "Well, I will tell you what I think, anyway. In my eyes, you are just like a piece of shit!"

The master simply smiled and forgivingly stayed quiet.

Seeing that his insult had fallen on deaf ears, he asked curiously, "And what do you think of me?"

The master said, "In my eyes, you are a nice man."

Hearing this remark, the officer left happily and bragged to his wife about the incident.

His wife said to him, "You conceited fool! When a person has a heart like a pile of dry shit, he sees everyone in that light. The elderly master has a heart like that of the nice man, and that is why in his eyes, everyone, including you, is nice."

Message

Surely, you would exclaim, yes, one does understand but easier said than done. It looks good in the story but when our ego in real life takes a beating, we don't even remember most of the time whether the word 'forgive' exists in the dictionary or not. We want to teach the person as ugly a lesson as we felt at that point of time.

Forgiveness has a very beautiful word attached to it, i.e., give. If we start giving in life, we shall certainly stop desiring things after a point of time as we will start getting everything before we think about it, yes it is the law of nature. No, no one is making you dream. You are welcome to the world of reality where you get without asking and that is when you start giving, but not everything you have. Certainly you shall only give what you have. You should give generously and wholeheartedly. But again I repeat, you don't have to give everything.

Yes, somewhere, you may have possession of negative thoughts that you don't have to give. At the same time, you don't have to retain the negative emotions and the feelings to yourself. Eliminate the negativism within through genuine positive giving that has the power to wipe off all the negatives that are inside you. Positive Giving is so powerful that it will not let any further negativism come into you.

True, you are right as earlier stated, 'it is simply said than done'. We tend to keep thinking and circumspecting things that we forget to act on. This includes both forgiving as well as taking revenge. Till the time, we don't forgive someone we think we should or take revenge, till that time we simply cannot get peace of mind. We keep mapping and regulating our lives and the lives of people close to us. It is alright to map one's life but controlling others life in it there is a big question mark. If others start deviating from what was thought by us for their good, we tend to get hurt. Moreover, if we are recommended to forgive him or her, we don't like forgiving that person for such a deplorable suggestion. We might not remember these thoughts a few months—years later.

The best way to forgive is to start *forgetting*. Surely, we have a number of courses on memory but these courses do not help us if we want to use them to nurture our negative thoughts and reactions by retaining them.

If you are ready to forgive, it means you believe in the Laws of Nature. These are laws that don't spare anyone no matter how intelligent man may think of himself. Laws, are equal for everyone. These laws are neither made by human beings nor controlled by them; yes, these laws are controlled by our heavenly father who is unbiased and who does not differentiate. You must believe that the person who is harming you or has harmed you would be punished by the law. This is for people who can't forgive. But at least you, in this way, can stop reacting to the negative things and save yourself from negative reactions. You are saving yourself from doing anything wrong and also from being punished by the laws of nature. Hence, *don't react negatively.*

We have to *accept* that every individual has his own rules of the game he plays and we have to accept each other's rules and play. If we start doing this, then we shall be more aware about their rules and our negative reaction towards them and their negative reactions towards us will start subsiding which will get replaced with mutual understanding and intelligence. Eventually, it will become a habit.

Why is it so difficult to forgive?

It is difficult to forgive because we want the other person to undergo the same pain and anguish which we have gone through. We believe that we are doing individuals good by punishing him, so that he does not dare do it to someone else. But do we realize that we tend to let go our near and dear ones escape from our punishing reactions, who selfishly hurt us and take us for granted as we take everything in our strides as sacrifice without speaking. (This is negative forgiving). We don't realize that we are fooling ourselves and in the long run spoiling our near and dear ones. We also don't realize that like we forgive, the outside world shall not forgive them the way we forgive our near and dear ones. In the same way, we don't like forgiving the outside world and their near and dear ones.

Negative forgiveness

Negative forgiveness is forgiving the undeserving. The individual is simply forgiven, without being made aware of his actions or in other words complaining in appropriately. It is something like letting guilty go scot free and making him repeat his mistake, time and again. It may be either because of your love towards that person or your fear of him or you did not want to spoil your mood by interacting with such an individual even though he has done wrong to you directly.

Attachment- This is the biggest impediment. It looks vague, how one can live without being attached in this world. Obviously one does not want to be any swami or yogi who is ready to leave this beautiful world. Let us confront this question with an open mind. Think about the closest relative/ friend that you lost and how you felt when you came to know that he was no more in this world. You would have to live the entire life without him. At that point of time, you would have exclaimed *"impossible*! How can I think of living without the departed soul ?" It would have been a feeling of your life coming to an end and the thought "I can't live anymore". And years later, how often do you remember that departed soul, without whom you could not have lived earlier.

This is what attachment does to us. It makes us believe that there is nothing hereafter and this is the only thing left in life, not realizing that the only thing permanent in life is change. When we are too attached to a thing, that time we are not Mr. XYZ but we are Mr. Attachment. We are that Mr. Attachment who is clouded with his present and thinks that the present is without change. He realizes that the person to whom he was so attached has hurt him. Then he becomes Mr. Hurt. The individual who has apparently hurt him, may not have actually done so. What actually hurt was the thought that the individual would never go against his decisions, without realizing that in reality, he was trying to rule the individual. When the individual refused to be ruled by him, it hurt him and he became Mr. Hurt.

If at all we are genuinely hurt by our loved ones, we tend not to say something strongly as we care for them. Hence, we forgive them without seeking our forgiveness. It is as if you are freeing the guilty even before letting them know the wrong they have done.

Out of love

This refers to any negative forgiveness which happens because of attachment but manifests in the form of love. This can be seen very often in mother-children relationships, where child goes scot free as no questions are asked by the mother.

In case of the girl child, the mother is protective, by making sure that she does not talk to strangers and she is safe and secure in every way. She should not go out at night etc. The rewards the girls get for doing this is that at home she can do any thing at home, e.g., continuously watching television or talking on the phone for hours at a stretch. Mothers tend to forgive them, either by mentioning it casually or overlooking the act of the child by consoling herself with the thought "at least the child is at home". In the case of boys they are allowed to do whatever they want with a pretension that they are being watched but nothing ever is said to them specifically. Finally it is the children who have their last say. Thus, it is the love that keeps both the, mother and father, overlooking the wrong doings of their children, not realizing that the same can become lethal for their children when they are mature.

To forgive their children without questioning them is also because of the blind and selfish love parents have for the children. It happens because mothers don't want to relate with the fact that their child can and do wrong. (As it reflects somewhere on the kind of person the parents are). They selfishly imagine their children looking after them in their old age with full dedication. Thus, while disciplining they do not want to spoil the rapport with their child (if some mothers disagree with me, I ask them to ask themselves, would they not like to stay and be looked after by their children when they grow old? The answer shall be, yes. It does not matter how modern and how different we may show ourselves towards the spouses but one thing is for sure, our demands have not changed though we pretend it does not matter to us. Also out of love, they convince themselves that their child is the most innocent and the neighbour's child is the most notorious among the children around. So we find that all the other children are notorious except our own child, which means some other mother thinks about the same child as notorious and his mother thinks he is innocent.

Unfortunately, parents forgive to be in the good books of the children. As the child starts growing, there is an unsaid competition between the parents as to whom the child is closer to. The child acts as an extra vote for the parents when they disagree. To be in the child's good books, they are forgiven easily and communicated how much are they loved, not understanding that it is not love but the poison in form of love that is being injected into the child.

Out of fear

"I will pretend nothing has happened or I know nothing about the wrong he has done. Otherwise, he will start showing his evilness towards me and surely I don't want to spoil my mood or relationship with him".

Surely wrong forgiveness is a sin and the person who forgives wrongly is punished by nature. This obviously does not mean that we start punishing everyone. It means that if someone has done wrong, he should be taken to task and this should be done either by complaining to his parents, relatives, friends, or the law.

Shyam, a great devotee of God would not say anything to any one. He used to forgive everyone for he thought that as nobody can escape sins, the guilty would be punished. He used to smile and walk away, and not saying anything. The result was he stopped thinking and became inactive in life. He wanted to live in the material world but like a sage and surely that was not possible, as every role that you choose in life should also come with an environment. That is why one does not see sages living a family life. They tend to go to isolated places far from the crowd and the material world.

But here was a man with lots of material desire but at the same time failing to act and just forgiving. The result was his life came to a standstill. He did not know what to do. He was in a state of indecision and confusion, which further resulted in depression. Whenever people would tell him that they were cheated by a particular individual, he used to add that he was also his victim. People would ask him, "Why did you not complain to the cops ?" He replied, "Because I had forgiven him but I am sure God will punish him."

We should not be like a man liberally forgiving people(especially your loved ones) who deserve punishment. We allow such people to make others like them as this is contagious. If you are cheated by someone, you will always look at people with doubt while dealing with them. Imagine if we don't punish the person who cheated on us, he will be cheating others and creating a doubt amongst others in the society. Such a society never has and never can have any future. Punishing here means doing it laughly or making the person aware about his undoings rationally.

But this also does not mean that one starts punishing each and everyone and most of the times wrongly. Generally, we want to punish those from whom we have taken to or whom we have sacrificed our interests. Hence, it hurts us most. Surely, we should tell them that we are not fools and we will like them to ensure that we recover our losses. But thinking single mindedly about ourselves and try to punish people who we think are at fault, though actually they may not be at fault is also a sin.

Ego

Sigmund Freud believed and quite correctly said that in time, ego channelises the psychic energy in a manner that leads to socially acceptable conduct. He believed that ego was rational, logical, and socially acceptable, as it rationalizes the interaction between the individual and the society. Its main task is to satisfy the impulse in a rational acceptable manner. He was born in 1856 and as they say, life is moving at a fast pace. Either the meaning of ego has changed or the way we look at it has changed.

Ego, which used to be thought about as rational at one point of time, is the cause of conflict and irrationalism that is spreading like fire. Today, life is mostly confined to ego. 'A' says "I shall not apologise. My ego does not permit me doing so". 'B' says, "I shall not forgive because you have not sought apology in the right manner." (B's ego wants the apology in its own way).

Positive forgiveness

Positive forgiveness is forgiving someone after attempting to make him realize his mistake and the aftermath that could have been harmful to him. You can't forgive unless someone seeks forgiveness. It may so happen that the other person was oblivious of the hurt. Hence, speaking to him and informing him about the same is necessary. Positive forgiveness has no place for violence, accusations, abusive, and foul languages. It is carried out in a subtle way without making a big issue out of it. At times, there are trivial things, which if not forgiven on time may take the shape of unexpected disaster, e.g., if someone is late, you don't complain and some day make an issue out of it by giving him lectures and invariably blaming him for things, which he may not have done just because you are upset with him. It also does not mean that you don't say anything to him from time to time. You just make a sincere statement that you have not liked what he has done as it has resulted in time loss and he should not repeat it in the near future.

The gesture should be sincere, otherwise you may not be able to concentrate on work for which you had called him up in the first place. You don't have to let the upset factor take over; otherwise the upset factor over the same thing will make you sad with continuous reaction. You may start feeling that you are unworthy of things and will pull down your self-esteem. The result is that such a small thing, which had made you lose your time initially has also ventured into your work efficiency, played with your concentration, and made you look like a fool in the end.

Forgive positively

Forgiving positively does not happen in life easily. People tend to show that they are liberal and strong at heart when it comes to forgiving through their expressions and body language. But there is always a difference between displaying our feelings and what one feels inside. In fact, the people who tend to show their strength of forgiveness when they are alone are the ones who would speak negatively and get into backbiting, which means that on the face whatever they have depicted was just superficial and they have not actually forgiven yet. This pretension of forgiving and reacting negatively is also as bad a sin as done by the person whom one is trying to forgive.

Experience of thief with a Zen master

One evening, Zen master, Shichiri Kojun, was reciting sutras when a thief entered his house with a sharp sword, demanding "money or life". Without any fear, Shichiri said, "Don't disturb me! Help yourself with the money, it's in that drawer". And he resumed his recitation. The thief was startled by this unexpected reaction, but proceeded with his business anyway. While he was helping himself to the money, the master stopped and called, "Don't take all of it. Leave some to help pay my taxes tomorrow".

Channelizing Self for Success

The thief left some money behind and prepared to leave. Just as he was leaving, the master suddenly shouted at him, "You took my money and you didn't even thank me! That's not polite!". This time, the thief was really shocked at such fearlessness. He thanked the master and ran away. The thief later told his friends that he had never been so frightened in his life.

A few days later, the thief was caught and confessed, among many others, his theft at Shichiri's house. When the master was called as a witness, he said, "No, this man did not steal anything from me. I gave him the money. He even thanked me for it." The thief was so touched that he decided to repent. Upon his release from prison, he became a disciple of the master and many years later, he attained enlightenment.

Message

Retaliation takes you to a similar behaviour, which injects anger and hatred in you and your actions are at a similar point. The Laws of Nature will surely punish the person who has wrongly troubled you. But you may get punished instead of getting the reward that could have been yours if you would have forgiven with a warning. One should forgive with a warning that ensures better confidence and self-esteem than the person who does not do it. Thus, it is important that you forgive with full satisfaction rather than cursing the other person covertly and forgiving him overtly.

The exercises given below will help you to relate with the forgiving self and help you to be with it.

When was the last time you had forgiven someone and why?

_____
_____
_____
_____
_____

Do you think you had an adequate reason for making the other person sorry?

_____
_____
_____
_____

If you had been at the other person's place, what would you have done? Explain.

_____
_____
_____
_____

Are you sure you are not becoming over-critical about others resulting in a negative approach?

_____
_____
_____
_____

Pen down three occasions when you have been forgiven? Do you think you deserved to be forgiven?

_____
_____
_____
_____

❐❐❐

Chapter 6

Assertiveness

Do you want to be—
- More Alive
- More sensitive
- More aware about yourself
- More aware about others
- More open to the feelings of others
- More confident
- More in control of your life than ever before
- A go-getter
- Having more profound relationships with more people

Then start practicing assertiveness. Assertiveness is listening to and taking out small or big genuine feelings (positive or negative) about others from time to time. It helps you to keep a healthy and positive relationship with people around, in general, and your loved ones, specifically. Most importantly nobody takes you for granted.

Though I said, taking out your feelings... in the above paragraph, I can say one thing with confidence that none of us are assertive all the time. We tend to choose and identify those with whom we can be assertive, aggressive and timid.

More often than not, we tend to feel so strongly about so many things around us but are unable to communicate 80% of them. Moreover, we then tend to punish ourselves for not communicating what we felt at that point of time.

And by then it is too late. The person goes and we are left behind with our feelings to ourselves. This is where assertiveness comes in, we express ourselves with pride and dignity so that we don't have to be ashamed and embarrassed with ourselves. Let us analyze your reactions with different individuals first.

Write down the name of people whom you dominate most of the time and why?

_____
_____
_____
_____
_____
_____
_____
_____

Write down the list of people who dominate you most of the time and why?

_____
_____
_____
_____
_____
_____
_____
_____

Mention the names of people with whom you are assertive and why?

_____
_____
_____
_____
_____

Obviously, the people with whom we tend to be aggressive are those about whom we do not have a very high opinion viz-a-viz their personality. We think we can dominate them easily in any way at any time. We tend to take them for granted and act with overconfidence with them. Secondly, the people with whom we tend to be assertive may not be many (negligible) in our lives as we tend to play a role either of dominance or timidity. Thirdly, we tend to get into our shell with people about whom we have high opinion. We take them to be more powerful and more successful than us, and we feel the need to be in their good books all the time, no matter what they say about us or the way they treat us.

No doubt, you want to be in the good books of some people but that does not mean you will allow them to dominate and control you. If you are allowing it, you are living in a fool's paradise. You think they are happy with you and will take care of you. But the fact remains that the impression you carry about people you dominate (a low opinion viz-a-viz their personality;) we tend to take them as fools and just another normal human being etc. is the same impression these people (those whom we envy) carry about you.

Suppose you are recruiting people for your company. Ramesh and Mahesh come for the interview. First, Ramesh comes in and you start interviewing him. Whatever you say, Ramesh agrees with you all the time. Ramesh keeps saying, "Yes sir, you are right sir. Surely I will do it this way. Yes sir, there is no other way of doing it" etc. What will be your impression about him? You might say, "Nice, polite, good man but if he goes on with this timid attitude, nobody will like it. The impression of my company will also go down. He isn't dynamic."

Then Mahesh walks in and he openly disagrees with you on some issues, and gives you reasons why he thinks otherwise. He gives you suggestions, which are different. You will surely like to keep him because you will find him a sharp and good communicator. Though you may like buttering which Ramesh did but at the end of the day you realize that you need smart people who have the ability to think divergently and not convergently for your company.

Aggressiveness

"He is very aggressive". You must have heard this statement quite often being used either for or by you. If it is used by you, think of the immediate image that comes to your mind about the person you are referring to. Is it negative? Surely it is.

In school, we have all type of peers. Right from the intelligent, creative, and sober to the extremely rowdy peers in our class who bully others and believe in violence. They are easily termed as aggressive. It may be so that they do not know how to communicate

without being rough with others. In other words, their style of communication is an angry face and aggressive body gestures, foul abusive language, and a sinister attitude.

Observation

Aggressive students are seen as
- Rowdy
- Ruffians
- Dominating- " No, we will go for a movie today."
- Introvert/ pretend to be introvert- " Yeah"
- Violent- " Your days are numbered."
- Making fun of others- "Hey look, he is always in the company of girls."
- Short tempered- "Be within your limits, else I shall teach you a lesson."
- Naughty- "Look at his body. Suddenly, he has started looking strong."
- Scheming - "Lets hide his tiffin-box."
- Boasting- "My brother knows that gangster. Stay away from me."

In the above list, you will not only see the aggressive peers at school but will also observe the contradiction in their behaviour. For instance, on one side, they are introverts or assume to be an introvert and on the other side they keep boasting. This paradox occurs because they become self-proclaimed leaders of the group. They assume that as leaders they should say only important things to an important person and at an important time. Hence, their followers keep talking and updating them with information about who is doing, what in school and his area. The self-proclaimed king/ leader keeps listening to what is being said, nodding his head from time to time. When it comes to boasting, the same person makes a sea change in his behaviour by boasting about his contacts and flexing his muscles to show his worth in front of his opposition, so that the others realize that he is too powerful for them and run away.

Also, if they don't like somebody, instead of telling them frankly why they don't like them or are avoiding them, they confront them alarmingly and threateningly. It may happen that the leader is right, as he believes he should not talk with the other person but his way of expression is obnoxious.

When they grow up, such individuals struggle in life because they are way behind others academically, as in their school days they had spent a lot of their time playing the fool and not studying. They are not able to keep pace with the world. But surprisingly it has also been seen that such people are also hard-workers and good salesmen as they grow up. However, the basic finishing is also not present unless and until such people voluntarily seek to change themselves.

Similarly, in offices we find people who are introverts, who will not communicate or will communicate, up to the point, will get rude and angry quickly and they will assume that they should be understood in a few words and there is nothing very important to elucidate. They tend to take people around them for granted and assume themselves as self-righteous.

In the office too, one finds colleagues who are-
- Moody- " Hi dear, how are you?" And the next time "you fool, what did you do?"
- Typically conventional " How can you celebrate target achievement in office in this manner" ?
- Rigid-"I don't change my decisions. What has been said, has been said".
- Introvert- " Yeah, ok, I will see, yeah."
- Get upset fast- Screaming "This wasn't the way I told you to do it."
- Angry- " Don't disturb me now. Get lost."
- Bad listeners- "Now listen to me, I have understood what you want to say."
- Self-righteous- "I know what I am doing and it's right."
- Self-praising- "What I said the other day has happened."

- Hypocritical- " My God, people in this office are lousy to work with."
- Kleptomaniac at times- " I will teach him a lesson." Starts planning how to do it.

These are basically inactive people.

But the imperative question here is whether these people are always bad, evil or wrong, or do their way of expression make them look that way. They might be very good individuals by heart, but the projection that is given to the outside world is that they are bad, short-tempered, and rough. The world believes that it is not worth talking to them. "If I say something, he just might get very angry", or "Why should I loose my peace of mind by talking to such a person?" etc.

If you have observed a politician, you will see that he will lie very cleverly and calmly in front of the camera and with people in general. A good soul, who confronts him may get so upset with the politician's bluff that he might become aggressive and start accusing the politician. The whole focus would shift from the key issue, which the individual was trying to depict to how the individual is talking. Secondly, the real life aggressive politician gets saved because he is not being aggressive.

When do we become aggressive?

We become aggressive when we keep storing things inside our hearts that have hurt us and feel strongly about. Over a period of time, these negative feelings that we have been harbouring inside surface and explode. As a result, the volume of negative feelings makes us look aggressive and ugly. We may have been right for all this while, it gives the wrong/ bad people an opportunity to justify that we are wicked as it can be seen from the way we talk. They get a chance to shift the focus from 'what we are talking to how we are talking'.

For example, 'A' tells 'B' that he could not come the other day because he had to go to his child's school. But 'B' thinks why 'A' did not call as he had kept waiting for him. 'A' had wasted 'B's time. Also 'B' felt ashamed that he had not been able to convey his true feeling to 'A', although he posed to be confident and strong from outside.

Two weeks later again 'A' had to visit 'B' at 14:00 hrs. This time he reached 'B's' office at 17:00 hrs and apologized immediately and started discussing the work with 'B'. 'B' thought why 'A' did not call and inform him that he was going to get late, and that he wasted 3 hrs. But again 'B' kept quiet and went on smiling as if it was ok with him. Again 'B' felt ashamed for not being able to communicate what he thought.

And the time went on with 'A' and 'B' not changing their respective attitudes. After a year, suddenly 'B' shouted at 'A' at the top of his voice about how 'A' dared to take him for granted and kept wasting his time. But when 'B' started accusing 'A', he started forgetting things and experiences to substantiate why and what he said. 'B' was at a loss for words and ideas and though he was right, at that point of conversation with 'A' he looked like a foolish child crying and complaining.

Result

'B' before exploding felt

- Resentful- (example)
- Anxious- " Why do I have to wait for 'A' every time?"
- Low self-esteem- "I don't think I can work without him."
- Dissatisfaction with self- " Why the hell can't I tell him to stop acting smart"?
- Limited amount of closeness- "What should I say or not say to him." He talks about what has to be done leaving his feelings in a lurch, as he feels what is to happen has already happened.
- 'A' to understand without actually telling him- " I should not say anything to him, otherwise our relationship will get spoilt. I hope he will understand soon."

- Uncomfortable with more people around him

'B' after exploding

- He could not express what he wanted to say in anger.
- People around were not convinced about him.
- 'A' also got the opportunity to shift the focus from what was being said to how it was being said.
- 'B' had a permanent broken relationship with 'A'.
- Thereafter, 'B' was convinced he had the poorest interpersonal skills in the world and his confidence level started going further down but this time at jet speed.
- 'B' got convinced that he was a misfit in the world as he was too nice to everybody and that was the reason others took advantage of him. He kept quiet all the time.

How did 'A' feel when he was doing injustice to 'B'?

- He thought 'B' was a fool.
- He told himself that he would keep on taking liberty with 'B' till 'B' kept digesting it and did not complain about it.
- He thought if 'B' would get angry too, he would be able to win over him.
- He took 'B' to be Mr. Nobody and thought about him only if he had work, whereas B kept thinking about him constantly.
- He thought he had become more confident.
- He saw he had the liberty to say whatever he wanted.

Caution

Nobody is asking you to become 'A'.

Certainly 'A' was unable to see that-

- People started hating him inwardly.
- They started talking about him behind his back.
- They started comparing him with the devil.
- They started cursing him.
- They were paranoid about him.

- They were subconsciously waiting to hear some untoward news about him.

What could 'B' have done here?
- If he would have told 'A' initially that this was not the way he expected to be dealt with and elucidated his point, it would have given a clear signal to 'A' and he would not have got late. Also 'B' 'S self-esteem would have been high and their relationship would not have been a broken one.

This is what assertiveness is all about. Listen to your feelings and don't forget to express them. Unfortunately, in this modern era we have been made to replace our feelings with thoughts, i.e., heart with the mind. "You should feel this way about it and not that way." Thus, an individual starts thinking that he has to feel in a particular manner as it is socially desirable. In this way, individual feelings start getting replaced by his thinking and over a period of time, he starts losing his feelings and hence, loses his identity.

- Concentrate on your feeling and not what others will think.
- You are as important as others.
- If others have the right to say what they feel, you also have an equal right to say what you feel.
- Don't overburden yourself by thinking how the other person will feel or think about you.
- If you have problem with a few people, then don't change yourself but improve as the scope for improvement is always there. However, if many people have a problem with you, then you need to change, not improve.

Assertiveness makes a person
- More alive
- More sensitive
- More aware about himself
- More aware about others
- More open to the feelings of others

- More responsible
- More time conscious
- More successful

Answer the following questions :—

Q. Have you been assertive or aggressive with the following people? Why?

1. Father

_____
_____
_____
_____
_____

2. Mother

_____
_____
_____
_____
_____

3. Siblings

_____
_____
_____
_____
_____

4. Friends

_____
_____
_____
_____
_____

5. Neighbour

_____
_____
_____
_____

Q. Briefly list five situations in your life where you would like to be more assertive and why?

1.
_____
_____
_____
_____
_____

2.
_____
_____
_____
_____
_____

3.
_____
_____
_____
_____
_____

4.
_____
_____
_____

5.

_____
_____
_____
_____
_____

1. I often become aggressive when

_____
_____
_____
_____
_____

2. My biggest fear of being assertive is

_____
_____
_____
_____
_____

3. The two people in my life that I find hardest to be assertive with are

_____
_____
_____
_____
_____

4. I am already quite assertive when

_____
_____
_____
_____
_____

1. You are a customer in queue waiting to be served during your busy lunch hour. Suddenly, a frail old lady steps in line ahead of you and claims that she is in a hurry. How would you feel and act?

_____
_____
_____
_____
_____

2. After walking out of a store where you purchased some items, you discover that you were short-changed by five rupees. What would you do?

_____
_____
_____
_____
_____

3. You are in a group discussion at work, which includes your boss. A colleague asks you a question about your work, but you don't know the answer. What would you do?

_____
_____
_____

4. You are in the middle of watching a very interesting television program when your partner comes in and asks you for a favour, which means missing the rest of the program. What would you do?

_____
_____
_____
_____
_____

5. A friend drops in to say 'hello', but is staying too long, preventing you from finishing an important project. Your friend is unaware that he is interrupting your work. What would you do?

_____
_____
_____
_____
_____

Assertiveness technique

What-When-How-Technique

One can start being assertive by questioning himself—

1. How am I feeling- Remember we are not talking about our thoughts here. Thoughts are different from feelings. They come from the head and feelings come from the heart. Therefore, identify your feeling, whether you feel good or cheated or have a mixed feeling. What are your feelings towards the other person : are they positive, negative or neutral.

e.g.:
If somebody tells you that you have not done some work right. How will you feel?
   (a) You may not like the statement because apparently, you are being criticized.

(b) You may either apologize since you have hurt someone, but why should you apologize unless and until you find out what has hurt the other person and whether he is fully aware about the facts or is jumping to conclusion.

(c) You may be rude to that person by being aggressive and how dare he say this to you.

(d) You might tell the other person that he has no right to accuse you on the first go. First, he should tell you the problem, seek clarification from you and then conclude his judgment.

2. When am I feeling- At times, it happens that individuals who are only concerned with their thoughts may not realize their feelings. It may strike them after the other person has left. In such cases, if you are supposed to meet him in a few hours, then you should wait not to give clarification but to ask why it was said. If you will not meet him shortly, then call him and enquire about it instead of sulking and punishing yourself.

3. Why am I feeling- It is very important to use your

discriminative faculty before accusing anyone. It may so happen that you accuse someone for something that he has not done, as we often believe that this world is revolving around us. We tend to measure everything with what is being said and done in respect to us.

But often we don't realize that it is our excessive attachment to ourselves and our needs that they have inflated our ego and make us feel selfish and self-centered. In such situations, our selfishness will take over our true feelings and the feelings we think of being true may just be superficial.

Self-Centered

Rakesh thinks that-

" Rishi was supposed to make a programme for a movie."

"Sushil will certainly call me up."

"Rita said that she would call me one of these days."

The first point I am trying to make is that we in general and Rakesh specifically expect others to fulfil their responsibility by thinking and doing special things for them.

The second point is, suppose if these people did not make a programme or call. How would we feel?

The imminent feeling would be of being hurt and cheated and being embarrassed and ridiculed, of not being called or thought about. How had Rakesh felt? The feeling of Rakesh will manifest into thinking negatively about Rishi, Sushil or Rita and accusing them of varied things not only what they had done recently but also things that they did earlier.

But suppose Rakesh comes to know that these friends could not call him up because Rishi met with an accident, Sushil was out of town for some immediate work, and one of Rita's relatives had expired.

Suppose, if without listening to his friend's genuine problem he had exploded. Imagine the result. To Rakesh, it would have been his true feelings being communicated not realizing that they were biased feelings far away from truth and reality. Rakesh kept on thinking negatively about his friends who were in a real mess at that point of time. How would you react if you came to know about this? You will feel upset with yourself.

Hence, minimize the chances of feeling upset with yourself / others.

If Rakesh had kept his ego at bay or under control and called up his friends-:
(a) He would have come to know about true situation very fast, and
(b) He would not have to go through negative feelings about his friends.

Remember biased feelings are not your true feelings. Never express them immediately; understand and then act. If, after understanding without being biased, you feel it ought to be expressed assertively, please do it. However, don't make a mockery of this word assertiveness without understanding your true feelings.

Having said this, to do well in life, one should be non-aggressive both physically and within and that is where assertiveness takes over.

CASE STUDIES

Case study I

"Son, you are a young man. I would like you to go out of station for three weeks, so don't worry about accommodation and food," the boss said. When the son reaches there, he finds that the accommodation is much below average and he has to live there for three weeks. What does he do?

First option- Call up his boss and tell him what an ugly accommodation he has got and he was coming back, if he does not get a decent accommodation.

Second option- Sit quietly, curse his employer for sending him to this hell and also curse himself because he does not have the guts to speak about the apparent injustice being done to him. Also satisfy himself with the thought that had he known he would have got this. He would not have ever come to this place (though there also he would not have had the guts to say anything as fear of losing job really haunts him and wait for the days to pass by though it will affect his results also".

Third option- " To use auto suggestions that may the wisdom of humanity prevail over my boss's mind".

Case study 2

Your boss has given you a task/assignment and has told you that you have to take all the decisions and he wanted the work done successfully. What do you do?

First option : You say to yourself, what problem has come on me? What if I fail? What if I am unable to take correct decisions? Thus, you start getting worried".

Second option : You feel good that you are in control of a job but when you start it, you are not sure what should be done. You try to think too much and do too little. All the time, you keep on thinking what decision your boss would have taken. Or, if you would have taken this decision in the presence of your boss how he would have reacted. What would he have told you? And you keep on going to your boss to inform him, so that, if tomorrow the thing does not work out, you can clearly tell him I was informing you all this.

Third option : You do everything that you believe is right and your decisions are taken on the basis of sound reasoning.

Fourth option : Call up the boss and try to tell him what he was going through, telling him in that environment the chances of getting good results (that was the reason for the boss sending him) will be not very profitable.

Case study 3

You have been delegated work and you are expected to show it to your boss the next day in the morning. You know that at home, it will take you at least 3 hrs

to complete that work. **Your friends visit and they ask you to have dinner and watch a movie with them. What will you do?**

Your true feeling- You feel tempted to go with them, since you have met them after some months. You have also been thinking of going for the same movie. Being your school friends, you also want to get nostalgic and you feel very happy and your real self when you are with them. What do you do?

Option I- You get carried away and decide that you will go with them and work when you return back, or get up early to do the same.

Option II- You criticize your boss that this was no way of asking you to do work at home. After all, home is meant for rest and enjoyment and not work. You are confused and vulnerable.

Option III- You refuse your friends by making them aware about the work load and the responsibility your boss has entrusted on you. That you may fix up some other day with them and that things don't work in short notices.

Keep practicing being more and more assertive and you will find a big change in your behaviour towards others and the behaviour of others towards you.

Chapter 7

Habits– only strong persons can change them

"Habits make a man weak". Habits programme the individual in such a way that the individual gets paralyzed in both mind and action when he sees a change. Habit formation happens with or without the knowledge of the individual. It may happen consciously or unconsciously. The chapters that you have already read are the guiding force for you to act consciously and in turn formulate conscious habits in your life.

But generally, this does not happen since we do not apply ourselves to gain the right knowledge which can constructively form our habits. By overlooking knowledge we allow habits to form destructive behaviour in our lives. Our behaviour comes from our habits and habits come from our knowledge and learning. How much we have learnt makes a beginning towards a constructive habit.

What is a constructive habit?

Constructive habit is consciously formed keeping in mind the well being, the desire to evolve and get success out of life. Constructive habit comes with a continuous effort of converting our negative behaviour into positive ones and eliminating our negative behaviour with knowledge and the implementation of that knowledge. Constructive habits are initiated only by individuals who are strong when they realize how important their inculcation means to their lives.

Constructive habit only happens when an individual is in touch with himself/herself. He often quietly assesses himself and softly comprehends the opinion and reactions others have towards him/her. Secondly, he evaluates the reactions and opinion by assessing whether those reactions are right and what people in general think about him/her. If the answer is yes, then he moves on to the third step by promising that he will change his behaviour, which is not socially desirable.

When exams are near, every individual tries to make a constructive habit studying at least during that period of time. No matter how much one has studied during or after the school but during this time, the realisation that one has to do well is present. Therefore, the constructive habit makes the individual's games/ hobbies/ interests areas take a back seat. Thus, the understanding to change helps the individual change.

Destructive habits

These habits are formed unconsciously with people who don't have control over the thoughts. Individuals who do not give time to assess themselves are responsible for unconsciously forming destructive habits. One should not think that since they are unconscious about them it is not their fault. Who unconsciously permitted habits to become destructive habits? Yes, it was you.

We might blame our parents, friends, teachers, and society but the fact remains that only we are responsible for our destructive habits. We have already seen this in Chapter one in detail.

Causes of destructive/negative habits

(A) **People believe that life will take its own turn–** and so will habits. Since people believe that they are not responsible for their negative habits, similarly, good people are also not responsible for their good habits. It happens by chance.

(B) **People are lazy–** They are lazy in assessing themselves, they are lazy in finding faults within; in observing their own behaviours, and others' behaviour towards them.

(C) **Environment–** Man's behaviour is also related to the environment he lives in as it plays a major part in converting a behaviour into a habit. In childhood, you were friends with boys who used to abuse and think notoriously. After being in their company for a month you also started abusing as if you could not express yourself without foul language. And look at yourself now. You have become a gentleman again since the time you have started working and got involved in your work. You don't remember those friends of yours and you are relieved that you quit their company at the right time.

(D) **Over-ambitious–** When a person is over-ambitious and his patience level is low, to attain success, he starts doing things that are wrong, e.g., lying, cheating others, and making fools of others. The result is, he lands himself with all the bad habits which result in people not trusting him and looking down upon him in the long run.

(E) **Under ambitious–** These people have no goal in life and no desire to improve themselves. They live life in vain. I won't say they are without any objective from the very beginning. No, that won't be true. But certainly after trying their hands at a few things and failing repeatedly, they just stop thinking about their lives and simply blame it on to their circumstances. What remains is an individual without any vision and hope of resilience in life.

(F) **Manifold objectives–** When we have too many things going on in our mind and when we want to achieve everything in a short span of time, it results in negative habits. I may want to excel in computers, but at the same time want to do something for the country by getting into politics. In addition, one may also want to write a book about things that he strongly feels about. Having so many objectives in one's mind and hoping to achieve those objectives in a short span of time results in different behaviour related to different fields and the frustration and impatience results in negative habits being formed.

What does one do with these old unwanted habits? Here is the answer to the question.

1. **Old unwanted habits must be identified first–** The habits that need to be kicked out of one's life permanently should be identified. Get to know them from your friends, colleagues, parents, relatives, precisely the people around upon. However, do not change a habit just because one person has told you to do so. You should find out by the reactions and opinions of others whether 75% of them agree that you should change your habits. If they do then you should go towards changing those habits. Another word of caution is never try to find out from those who have similar bad habits.

For example, a drinker asks a group of drinkers whether he should quit drinking. The obvious response would be 'no'.

Identify five habits that you want to change?

1. _____

2. _____

3. _____

4. _____

5. _____

2. Why do you want to change the habit? – Imagine someone telling you that it is better to get up early and study instead of studying till late at night. And he further goes on to say that is the time most people study. You have tried getting up early to study and it just does not happen with you. Also, you study well at night. So, should you change your habit of getting up early and studying even just because 75% people around you say so? No, Never do that. Use your intellect because if your body is not ready for it and since it is the same thing whether you study early morning or late night, the objective is to understand your subject well rather than to make others happy by agreeing to do what they say.

Hence, always question yourself and find out whether the unwanted habit that you have identified, is actually unwanted. I am sure your intellect and conscience will never guide you wrong. Drinking frequently is bad and if a drunkard is trying to say he should drink because his intellect/ conscience is asking him to do so, then he is lying. It is his uncontrollable desire and habit that are compelling him to drink. And that is why such people in the first place are not ready to accept that they are doing something grossly wrong.

Why do you want to change these habits?

_____
_____
_____

3. Accept that you want to change the unwanted habit for good. You will have to mentally and repeatedly accept that the negative habit, which is a part of you, has to be thrown out of your system. You will have to accept it as serious as a cancer or a tumour, which

will make your life painful and short. So there is no middle way. Either you keep it in your system and suffer, or do away with it by eliminating it from your life. You are now getting mentally ready to knock the unwanted habits off. Keep thinking about the loss that you have incurred due to these unwanted habits. You should analyze how you have been put into difficulties by them and how, at times, you had to be embarrased because of this habit. Think how this habit has created more enemies and has driven away the good people from your life. Think about how it has driven away the love and care others had for you and you had for them. Think about how it has taken away the most special thing of your life with which you, at one time, could not imagine such negative relationship. Strongly accept that now this demon has to go for good.

Have you accepted that you want to change those habits? How?

_____
_____
_____
_____

4. Be ready to throw it out of your system– Asking you to be ready to throw it out of your system means that initially you should be ready for the sufferings and pain that you will undergo to eliminate it out of your system. A smoker should be ready to accept that the habit which he had for the past 20 years will not disappear easily. And he has announced that he will fight till the time he becomes victorious. Hence, you are both mentally and physically ready to get rid of unwanted habits.

Till what extent are you ready to go throw undesired habits out from your system?

_____
_____

Channelizing Self for Success

5. Analyze how often you get this unwanted habit– A smoker may smoke twenty two cigarettes a day. So, we have to keep a count on our unwanted habit. A person may drink in the evening everyday or at least 5 days in a week (People generally don't drink on Tuesdays and Thursdays in our part of the world, because of religious belief and obligations).

Be specific in assessing how many times this unwanted habit happens with you on daily/ weekly/ monthly basis.

_____
_____
_____
_____

6. What is the frequency of your unwanted habit?– Frequency helps us realize how attached we are to the undesirble behaviour.

How much time do you take in doing your unwanted habit ? Is it for a few seconds/ minutes/ hours?

_____
_____
_____

Also analyze whether the frequency varies or is it uniform.

_____
_____
_____
_____

If it varies, try and see why or under what circumstances ?

_____
_____
_____
_____
_____

7. What are the feelings that you get when you perform your unwanted habits?– Is it a sense of achievement, happiness, relief or confidence? You will have to identify the feeling that gives you pleasure and happiness, which stimulates you to repeat the undesired behaviour again and again.

   Identify what attitude you carry at the time of the undesired habit?

   _____
   _____
   _____
   _____
   _____

   Do you get the same feelings all the time or do they keep changing? Also find out that at times when you get the negative feelings try and see the circumstances when you get them.

   _____
   _____
   _____
   _____
   _____

8. In what situations do you get the undesired habits– Man is incomplete without the environment. Environment has a role to play directly/ indirectly in his behaviour. It becomes imperative for the individual to understand his environment so that

he can control the environment to some extent and with it his behaviour. Hence, there is the need to understand deeply the kind of environment/ circumstances/ situations that compel you to behave in an unwanted manner. For example, an individual may smoke frequently when he is alone. So the cause of the problem is being alone. If the individual wants to quit smoking, he should not be alone. In free time he should either go to a non- smoker friend's house or for a movie somewhere where he does not get the urge to smoke and his opportunities to smoke will be limited.

Write down the situations/ circumstances that happen just before you perform the undesired behaviour?

_____
_____
_____
_____
_____
_____

9. **Control the situation–** After identifying the situation, the only option left with you is to control what happens just before the undesired behaviour. If you are serious about it, you will have to draw the courage of doing something difficult but not impossible. Yes, the time has also come to check your seriousness, so that you know how serious you were? What is your character like? And can you achieve success in the future through this seriousness and character or not?

It is your responsibility to see that such situations and circumstances do not come that force you towards the undesired behaviour. Do not blame your friends, peers, parents, relatives, society etc. for the behaviour. If you get angry often, the onus lies on you to check the circumstances when you are unable to control your emotions and show aggression. You will also have to check your assertiveness skills, if you get angry.

How do you think you can control the situations that lead you to the undesired behaviour?

_____
_____
_____
_____
_____

Punishment– If you are unable to keep the promises of controlling your habits, then you will have to start punishing yourself. You should make a commitment to yourself that if you are unable to control the habit, you will not see a particular movie, which you wanted to see or you will not go out with friends or you will not go to the club for a week. These are some of the ways through which you can regulate the unwanted habits, which refuse to be eliminated.

Channelizing Self for Success

If you are unable to control the habit, the way you had thought, how do you punish yourself?

_____
_____
_____
_____
_____

Reward– Punishment is the key solution for the poeple who want to do away with the unwanted habits. But one has to reward oneself if one is able to control his habit even temporarily. You will have to decide both the rewards and punishment that you will get if you are not able to do the needful.

What are the rewards that you have given to yourself, and how do you feel after achieving them?

_____
_____
_____
_____
_____

I am sure you must know by now the scientific method involved with changing habits. You must have realised that instead of waiting for hope or time to do the needful, you have the better option of getting after it and achieving what you had previously only hoped. Now we move on to the final destination, Why are we doing all this? How will it help us in the future? How will it give us the decisive edge over others?

By now through all these chapters you have come to know what you have to do and why you have to do it. In this chapter, you have been told how it has to be done. But this is not all. Ask yourself why you are looking for improvement in the self. Surely it cannot be confined only to your good, because it has to be passed on to the company you work for and the nation you live in. In the next two chapters we will see why and how you got to think and work towards the above mentioned things.

❑❑❑

SECTION - III

ATTITUDE Traits
Applying the Tips and Techniques in real life

Chapter 8

Organizational Skills

Experience of blind followers

There was once a man who formed a religious cult and people regarded him as a very learned person. He had a few followers who recorded his instructions in a book. Over the years, the book became voluminous with all sorts of instructions recorded therein. The followers were advised not to do anything without first consulting the holy book. Whenever the followers went and whatever they did, they would consult the book, which served as the manual in guiding their lives. One day when the

Channelizing Self for Success

leader was crossing a timber bridge, he fell into the river. The followers were with him but none of them knew what to do under the circumstances. So they consulted the holy book.

"Help! Help!" the Master shouted, "I can't swim."

"Please wait a while Master. Please don't get drowned," they pleaded. "We are still searching in our holy book. There must be an instruction on what to do if you fell off a wooden bridge into a river."

While they were thus turning over the pages of the holy book in order to find out the appropriate instruction, the teacher disappeared in the water and drowned.

Message

The important message of the story is not to become slaves to any thought or book, otherwise you will never be able to progress in life, especially professionally. The only permanent thing in this world is change and we have to not only accept that change but to comfortably get involved in it. We no longer can live in this world with fixed notions and ideas and think of achieving success in life. If we apply the thumb rule, then we shall become redundant sooner than later in this modern era.

Dogmatism and narrow-mindedness should be thrown out of our lives if we want to progress in any organization; otherwise, without any organization to work with, one cannot achieve success. We should take the enlightened approach and not slavishly follow outdated conservative ideas, nor resort to any holy or management book without using our common sense, capabilities, and potential. In the face of changing circumstances and new discoveries and knowledge, we must learn to adapt ourselves, and respond to them by using them for the benefit of everyone.

After going through the initial chapters of the book, I suppose you would have started changing yourself for good. Now we come to the stage where with all the positive attitude, thought and learning, we come to the critical point of our life, where we use/ implement all these resources in our day-to-day life frequently, especially using these in the business environment persistently, till they become a part of us in the form of habit. The business environment, which is full of new unexpected challenges, needs a lot of endurance and expertise to deal with. Through the story, the message conveyed to you is to consolidate yourself, learn more and accept things that make you better and stronger in your path. But don't try to pick up things that move you away from your understanding of life. Add good things and keep subtracting negative things. Never subtract positive things, otherwise your life and personality will disintegrate.

Hence, to excel in your business/ professional life, there is a very important word floating these days called customer-care. Yes, customer-care has become a priority for every company and they continue to excel and improve their services vis-a-vis the customers, so that they can be more acceptable with the customers and increase their profitability with satisfaction.

Easier said than done. Surely, companies have made Human Resource departments with the view and understanding that if they keep the employees happy, the employees will be in a better position to serve their customers. Surely the intention is good. At last the business world is understanding the need to look after their employees, though it still may be for selfish reasons. The employees are getting the benefit though by default. The business community world-wide has realized that their employees can only make them grow and for that to happen, they have to take good care of their employees. The beginning has been made to be good and do good and in turn make money, but this is just the beginning.

Needless to say, individuals and companies tend to say a lot more than what they actually do. HRD concept was introduced worldwide by the west to take care of their employees and to treat them with respect, dignity and to give them what they deserved. In reality I don't see that happening at the moment. I don't see the employees coming back to homes on time, as they are delegated work of two people. What they get in return, a salary of 1.5 individuals with which initially they are happy and comfortable. Surely, it is a win-win situation for both the company and the employees, but honestly evaluating, it is not a healthy win-win situation. In fact, it is a forced win-win situation. Forced because to an individual looking for a job, 1.5 percent job is not offered to him but imposed on him. Imposed because the only option with him is either to take it or reject it. Especially in a country like India, most people cannot think of rejecting a job, which is again a sad state of affair.

Understandably things might sound pessimistic to you. Underpaid, six/ seven days a week, insult, humiliation, tension, botheration, but this is how millions of people are living and working. In spite of all these trials and tribulations, successful people come out every day, from these difficult situations in life and find adulation around. This is something like *sona ko jitna tapaoge utna nikharta hai.* (The more you heat the gold, more will it shine and glow). People who are successful in their endeavour are like gold who deserve every single moment of their success. And so you have got to be one in a million, who have to make a mark and shine like gold. You shall certainly come out victorious in spite of the said problems because if the others can do it, then so can you. The paranoma of success and recognition is wide in an organization. Every individual has an equal chance of getting it. But one needs to ask himself with full sincerity, "Do I need it?" And if you do, with what sincerity are you working towards it.

Learning or imbibing qualities are not good enough, when you go out to play the decisive game of your life, where you may come out as either a winner or a loser. Sure, life will give you a lot of chances and shall test you on decision-making skills. But a strong, pure clear thinker will never fail in any organization because he was living a life that had no pretense in it.

In every organisation, there are two types of customers namely the External Customers and the Internal Customers. An individual with his innate duty to look after both the types of customers cannot survive in this world. One has to respect both the external and the internal customers, if one has to succeed in life and that is not easy. Here, not only the internal respect is important towards both the customers but also how it is communicated from one's heart perfectly without creating/ minimizing any errors or miscommunication. Why the term heart has been used here is because you can touch millions of hearts through your heart but you cannot touch those millions with your mind. This is something a lot of companies have started realizing. Therefore, the word 'empathy' is in demand these days.

Who are these Internal Customers?

Internal Customers are the people who are working with you within the organization. They can be your boss, colleague, subordinate, or people from different departments like Marketing, Finance, Accounts, Human Resource, and Production, to name a few.

One deals with them almost on a daily/ monthly/ annual basis. One has to ensure that they are happy with us, if not totally with our performance, and the way we are working towards it. No one is suggesting here that one has to butter and keep his immediate boss or others happy. However, respecting their queries and answering them on time without hiding or being afraid of them and working towards building a long-term relationship with them, is highly important. If you can keep your internal customers happy, it shall bring in confidence in you, to take on your competitors, as you know that there are people back at the office who are always there with you.

Therefore, it becomes imperative on us to see how well we can keep our boss happy and satisfied, not by inflating their egos but by giving them a good sound performance. This can be done through achieving our targets and bringing new dynamic ideas that are workable and profitable in the current scenario. We have to work hard most of the time and work smart at times. It should not be vice-versa, otherwise you can put yourself in a fix, as working smart is also understood to be, like fooling others.

It happens at times that in office if you find people who you would love to hate, but you have to change your attitude by taking it up a challenge, to love them; not to avoid them or get irritated. You should try to eliminate the differences one has with them, by going to the root cause of it. This will not only increase your and their respect towards you, but the respect of the entire office towards you.

The External Customers

The External Customers are those because of whom our organisation was founded, is running and we have a job in hand. These external customers are being served by our organization and it is our responsibility to keep them satisfied and happy with our products and services, so that they don't go elsewhere. In a competitive environment, our competitors are waiting for us to make one mistake, so that they can capitalize on it by drawing our customers towards them, which would be our loss and their gain.

Today, companies are doing everything to keep their customers happy, which will give them more reasons to be in business. Companies go to the extent of fighting and cajoling the government to reduce various taxes so that their products become more affordable and more people can purchase them. Companies today are playing on volumes, the higher the volume, higher the profits. Essentially, to play in volumes requires voluminous customers.

In fact, the internal customers are in business because of the external customers and as far as we are concerned, we have to see that we can keep both of them happy, if we want to grow in an organization and thereby grow in life.

Normally, I have seen employees, customer care executives, their team leaders and managers, though they are supposed to be empathetic, are either genuinely not empathetic or they have no other option but to pretend to be empathetic. Probably that is the reason that companies no doubt, are spending millions of dollars/ pounds in training their employees, (I will not like to mention here rupees because I don't think Indian companies actually spend on training programmes) on the said skills.

Customers are dissatisfied at their end and companies at their end. Customers blame the companies openly but companies secretly curse the customers, of course, they can't afford to say it in the open. The result is there is a high rate of dissatisfaction within but the picture generally shown is of utmost satisfaction, as if the satisfaction level could not have been better than what it is.

The employees who do not have the innate ingredient of character towards people in general find themselves misfit with such a job wherein they have to take care of the customers. All I am-saying is that the pretension game that is being played in the corporate world is uncalled for. This is the reason I would want you to actually do what you do, so that no day, hour or minute you have to pretend and be ashamed of yourself. At home, people are rude but here in customer care people are compelled to behave themselves. (Once again no one is suggesting here that if you are rude at home, always remain rude but change habits). Obviously, overtly, nobody would come to know but covertly also you have to be is someone who is exactly the same.

The intention of the corporate world is very good but the implementation is not there. And in such situations/ circumstances as told to you in the first few chapters of this book, if you learn and implement them, then success will be a part of you in no time. If you are comfortable with your work, you are comfortable with the self and, by being comfortable with the self, you are raising yourself to the position of taking up new challenges and enhancing your creativity.

What is being suggested here is that if you are sincere, hard working, good from inside, you may already have further improved. Also, if you are being taught the ways of customer care you will only shine and be recognized. But if you are greedy, jealous, bad, rude, indifferent etc. from inside and you are polished with white (sincere, hard working, good, love, affection, care) in the office, you will turn into gray which means that your habits would be totally different while in office and at home . This may also lead to personality clash and, make you feel sad and worse than before, as you are trying to be different than what you are.

Let us now understand more about customer care and keep analyzing side by side how it comes naturally to you. If it does not come naturally to you, you don't have to be disappointed; you have to make a sincere effort to turn self from black to white, so that you are comfortable wherever you work.

- A customer is the most important individual for the company. He may or may not be in direct contact with you. He may come to you in person, may write to you or call you up and discuss his needs with you. His needs are of top priority for him and your need is to fulfil his need with utmost satisfaction. These questions will help you to find out your empathy level and how it can help you professionally.

How good are you at discussing other people's needs and why?

_____
_____
_____
_____
_____
_____

How good are you in discussing the needs of people you love and enjoy with and why?

_____

How good are you in discussing the needs of people who you think are of no use to you and why?

- We are dependent on the customer and surely the customer is not dependent on us because he has many options. However, we have him as the only option. As an employee or an employer we don't have any option but to take care of our customer, make him blossom so that in turn we too blossom with him. We cannot let the ego come, in-between the customer and us because in that case, we would be the losers and eventually our ego.

Do you think you are dependent on this world? Explain with reasons.

- Never think that a customer interrupts us in our work. On the contrary, he is giving us an opportunity to serve him. Life for the employee tends to become boring and monotonous after a while. Something that was seen as challenging and exciting once upon a time, has sadly become monotonous, probably because we have mastered it and now crave for something challenging and different. The result is that what the source of our bread and butter is, the job starts becoming an impediment, problem, and interruption in our lives. We tend to forget that it is because of our work that we are leading a good and happy life and we tend to neglect the job and making ourselves feel that it is not of much importance to us.

- A customer is not someone with whom you should argue. No problems have been solved with arguments ever. Arguments leave bad taste, negative energy, which further expands and also makes us evil. Also, at the same time no one is suggesting that the customer is always right. But instead of argumentation one has to be assertive and clearly communicate what one wants to communicate without being diplomatic and also without lying in form of false promises etc.

My Experience with a Multi National Company (MNC)

I would like to share a small experience, which happened with my aunt, and I was also a victim of it to an extent. My aunt came from a reputed international airlines of Canada, though it was a connecting flight from Canada. When she had to go back to America via Canada she fell sick at the airport and started puking there. Doctors were called and they gave her medicine and said she would be all right in some time and hence, she could fly non-stop for 15 hrs to Canada. But eventually she was off-loaded not because she was not well, nor because she had vomited but that she was carrying extra luggage. She called me from the airport and I went to pick her up. When she reached back home she started puking continually and a day later she was admitted to the hospital with dehydration. Food poisoning had happened to her and still doctors said she could fly such a long flight. Later she told me that she was literally thrown from the airport in that condition.

But that was not the end. It was just the beginning of her torture by the company which propagates Customer Care and by the employees who are supposed to empathise with the customer. I went to the airlines office in Delhi the next day on her behalf and told them the story. But they pretended they did not know anything about it and said the flights are full for at least next 45 days. When I retorted, they said they couldn't do anything as almost everyday they have been off-loading people from the flight. Though at that time I did not understand, later I came to know that in an airline if there are 300 seats they can do 20% more booking, i.e., there are 300 seats and 360 passengers have been issued tickets. And at that time also I thought what is this customer care. This is more like customer torture where everyday at least 60 people go disappointed as they don't know what these customer care executives are up to.

When I said that it was wrong, they said it was a worldwide practice. Hence, it is right. Are we trying to say here that if we make a policy where a few people can cheat and every time they cheat, they actually don't cheat because it is a policy? I know this is a relatively long story though it may be a story of a few minutes for you but think of the persons, days and hours when he had to go on with such a mess.

Then I asked the executives if they could give her a jumper seat and they replied they didn't have jumper seat in their aircraft. I thought that it was the joke of the century. They were polite but with politeness came unjustifiable policies, claims and lies. Eventually, my aunt went after 15 days but that too not by this airline.

Message

Tomorrow, you may run a company of your own or may work in a reputed company. No matter where you work, you will have to ensure that you work for your customer sincerely and try to find out a solution. Give genuine promises instead of temporary promises, as temporary promises are an eyewash that are never met.

Also, I want to communicate to all the Directors, CEO, COO, Presidents, and Chairmen of all the companies worldwide not to pretend to satisfy your customers, if you have such unfriendly policies for them.

I can go on and on with so many experiences. I can easily write a book with my own experiences and that too with corporate world. I am not stating facts just to gain sympathy or to increase the number of pages of this book but to tell you, people like these never rise in life and if they do, the way they rise in the same way they fall. I am sure you would not want to be cursed by others; so be with truth, decency and be undiplomatic, if you want others to sincerely respect you. People have become bored of these false and diplomatic versions and they have no time to listen to your diplomacy. They want you to come to the point.

- Never consider that a customer is a cold statistic though normally that happens. After a while, repeatedly listening and answering the same questions and giving the same answers. Moreover, seeing the customer data right in front of the table, one starts treating customers more as data than a human being. And this happens in all professions. I am sure, whenever you have visited hospitals and seen nurses treating patients not like human beings but some objects, without realizing how is he feeling; whether or not he is feeling any pain?

What is your perception of making profit?

_____
_____
_____
_____

Profit- customer retention

Profit is closely related to retaining the customer. If you and your company have influence on the existing customer over and over again, by giving him satisfaction with the product and the services, he will always come back to you. You have given your customer enough reason and confidence to come back to you again and again. As a result, your company will keep getting returns from the customer in the form of purchasing goods and services without actually investing them back on the customers regularly.

Retaining the customer means you are keeping him interested in your company and the product. This also means lesser spending on publicity, which will increase the profits of the organization while reducing the costs.

Faith and trust creates an immediate impression both for good or bad. If the customer is not happy and satisfied, he will never come back to you and your company again. On the contrary, if the customer has positive faith, he will always come back to you and in the long run this faith will get converted into trust.

Find more about you as a professional by answering questions, given below.

Which was your first job and how was your rapport with the Internal and External customers. Explain?

_____
_____
_____
_____
_____
_____
_____

If you haven't started working, yet you must at times have been given a task to perform with a lot of responsibility. How was your relationship with the person who gave you the task to perform and with the people on whom this task had to be performed?

_____
_____
_____
_____
_____
_____
_____

If you are working, what is your current analysis of yourself by their reactions, i.e., satisfaction of both internal and external customers?

_____
_____
_____
_____
_____
_____

What can you do for the betterment of the relationship with both the internal and external customers?

_____
_____
_____
_____
_____
_____
_____

❑❑❑

Chapter 9

Your National Duty

An experience of king Monkey

There was once a kingdom of monkeys in the forest. The King of the monkeys was very large, kind and wise. One day, the King was strolling and he noticed mango trees along the side of a river. He also noticed a human castle downstream. He then ordered the monkeys to remove all the mangoes from these trees, "or there would be disaster". The monkeys did not understand the King's intention, but they did as told. All the mangoes were taken off these trees except one. This one was hidden behind a nest.

Channelizing Self for Success

One day, this mango was ripe and fell into the river. It flowed downstream where the human King was having a bath. He noticed the mango and asked the Prime Minister what it was. The PM told him it was a "mango", a fruit of wonderful taste. The King then ordered that the mango be cut into small pieces and he gave a small piece to each of his ministers. When satisfied that the mango was not poisonous, he ate the rest of it and realized how tasty it was. He craved for more.

The next day, the human king and his troops, went upstream to search for more of these fruits. There were lots of mango trees, but also lots of monkeys. The human king doesn't want to share the mangoes with the monkeys, so he ordered all of them to be killed. A massacre started.

When the news reached the wise Monkey King, he commented, "The day has finally arrived". Thousands of monkeys were chased all the way to the edge of the forest. There was a deep cliff at the edge of the forest, and a bamboo forest at the other side of the cliff. The Monkey King saw that if his subjects could cross over to the bamboo forest, they will be saved.

With his huge body, he formed a bridge over the cliff and thousands of monkeys trampled over him to reach the safety of the bamboo forest. He endured all the pain. One monkey, who did not like the King saw this as an opportunity to get even. As he was crossing over the King's body, he pierced a spear through the King's heart. The King screamed but endured the pain until all his subjects were safely across. Then he collapsed.

The human king witnessed the whole thing. He was so touched that he ordered the Monkey King be saved. When the Monkey King recovered his consciousness, the human king asked him, "You are their King, why did you bother to endure so much pain for them?". The Monkey King replied, "Because I am their King". With that, he died.

The human king was so touched that he decided to be a good king from that day and he ordered that the monkeys in the bamboo forest be protected from harm forever.

Message

We have duty towards ourselves, our family members, friends and acquaintances. We have to evolve and perfect ourselves. We have to be more optimistic in our thoughts and approach towards life. We have to analyze ourselves every time. All these efforts have to be done as a matter of gratitude and respect towards the nation we live in. The country, which has given us air to breathe, freedom to live and education to excel. We certainly have our obligation towards it, no matter how positively/ negatively we feel about it.

If we grow, the nation grows with us, due to us and if the nation grows we also grow because of the nation. Hence, we have to keep this always in our mind that the opportunity to create and excel is not only provided by our employer or the customers, but the base has come from the infrastructure and facilities that our country has provided us with. Therefore, we have to further strengthen that base (country) so that the base in turn strengthen us and our future generations.

We often tend to live for ourselves from childhood. We want particular toys to play with, food to eat, places to go and people to meet. If we get fixated towards ourselves by any means then we tend to become more rigid and less flexible. We tend to be self-centred and always think about ourselves.

The result of such an act is when we grow and if we think more about ourselves, with friends in particular and society in general, we start loosing them. Similarly, if we think about our own growth in the organization, the people in the organization start ignoring us unless and until we come out with something spectacular. At the macro level, if we start ignoring the nation, the nation starts ignoring us.

I do believe that there are many things that have to be sorted out within our country . But that does not mean till the time these things are not sorted out, I shall not love or work for my country. We must realize that there can be no end to obstacles and problems as they are a part of life, manifested because of us and the solution for all these things also lies in us.

Understandably, our country has been governed by illiteracy, corruption, selfish- vested interest, uncaring behaviour, and self- centredness. All these things are the reasons that we have always been ruled. First, we were ruled by the Mughals and then by the Britishers and since 1947, I have no shame in accepting that we have misruled our nation because of already stated negative innate qualities.

As a matter of fact, I believe that families that were working under the Britishers have very comfortably been able to raise their standards of living but subtle miseries also have arrested them which is intangible for the outside world. This is because they have forgotten that the Laws of Nature are at work. However, the real people who sacrificed and struggled for the freedom of this country, are the real victims even today. Now one might exclaim, that is why it is important to be always self-centered, but I can tell you that self- centered people are cowards, and these are the people who eventually live an average life. That is why they or their families never succeed in life.

Why do you think that the Britishers were able to rule us for over a century? It was because our personalities were of submissiveness and immediate comfort was our aim. Not more than 1% of people took part in the real freedom struggle. Everybody wanted freedom, but they thought why should they go and revolt when others are not doing it or, since others are already revolting then why should I risk my life unnecessarily.

You certainly cannot grow in life if you desire to succeed only for the self. Success will come to you only if you think about your responsibilities towards the world and the country you are part of. Also, when you start understanding your responsibilities towards your country, then the success is imminent, it is only a matter of time. But people just think about themselves; their interests are just confined to themselves and as the result their thoughts are small. With small thoughts if one can imagine of success in this world, then I can only pity such people. I think of it as no more than just another dream. Hence, if you wish to become big, start thinking big and of course, there is nothing bigger than the universe. If we start thinking about the universe and our responsibilities towards it, we cannot be small.

This world and more specifically our country has a lot of problems. The main reason of this problem is the manpower or the people. The kind of people a country has, the kind of attitude and the aptitude they carry, is the kind of government or rulers they get. If the people of any country are corrupt, evasive, selfish, and self-centred, then the government of that country would also be selfish, evasive about important matters concerning the same people, corrupt by thoughts and actions and will try to earn undeservingly through short-cut methods, and last but not the least, selfish. The people will be responsible for both the cause and the effect and they will be the oppressors and the victims and this will all happen because of lack of knowledge.

Once I was talking to highly educated professionals and I asked whom they would vote for in the Tamil Nadu assembly elections, whether it would be AIADMK or DMK. Unanimously and promptly came the reply AIADMK because Jayalalitha, the yesteryears heroine was good looking once upon a time. Now, if we have educated people who have the discriminative faculty but still do not like to use them and vote like illiterates, where can such a country go?

Also, in the 2004 general elections all the political parties focused on filmstars and made them stand in the elections. People like Govinda, Smriti Malhotra, Dharmendra, etc. who do not have any experience of politics swore to serve the country, by standing in the elections. Some of them won comfortably. This is a matter of disgrace. Once in Shekhar Suman's show Smriti Malhotra was invited and since she was campaigning for the BJP, she was asked a few questions by Shekhar Suman, e.g., in how many states was the BJP ruling and such related questions. She did not know these basic answers and she was representing the party at the national level !

Then there is the dynasty rule. This country has been ruled for more than 40 years not by Congress but by the Gandhi Family. We talk very conveniently about democracy but are we living in true democracy. Is this the real democracy? You can start counting : in Haryana you have Chautalas and Bhajan Lals, in Bihar you have Laloo Yadav and his wife the Chief Minister and pointless talking about what she can do. Similarly, in all the states you will find dynasty rule. Thus, we have to accept the fact that few people are ruling this country because we are not being responsible to our motherland. Then how can we be responsible to ourselves?

The issue of foreign origin, whether it is an issue or not, I will not discuss. But I can say one thing very confidently, with the kind of attitude we have in this country even Bill Gates, Bill Clinton, George Bush, John Major, anyone can come and win elections from selective seats. Then efforts will be made to convince us that they have been accepted by the people of this country.

Experience of you and me

Lawyers - NASA was interviewing professionals to be sent to Mars. Only one could go and that person couldn't return to Earth.

The first applicant, as an engineer, was asked how much he wanted to be paid for going.

"One million dollars," he answered, because I want to donate it.

The next applicant, a doctor was asked the same question. He asked for two million dollars.

" I want to give a million to my family and balance for the advancement of medical research."

The last applicant was a lawyer. When asked how much money he wanted, he whispered in the interviewer's ear, "Three million dollars."

"Why so much more than the others?" the interviewer asked.

The lawyer replied, "If you give me $ 3 million, I'll give you $ 1 million, I'll keep $ 1 million, and we'll send the engineer."

Message

Certainly, one should resist such ideas no matter how clever and smart one may be. You should be a man of integrity and believe in making honest money. If you are not making money honestly, you are either stealing the share of people around you or the share of the nation. In both cases, you cannot escape no matter what you think about yourself. One should stand for something one believes in and that belief should be pure and should concern others.

The scenario is bad but all is not yet lost. We need to have resilience to come out of all this. And if we can hope to make the difference to firstly the universe, and then to our nation, we will automatically make a difference to our lives.

If you are thinking about something big you will get the insight about big ideas and that will further give you opportunity to work on that idea. What action can you take without an idea?

But if you are only thinking about yourself in this universe and the ways of becoming popular, achieving fame and wealth, then because you are only a drop in this big ocean, you shall be lost. If you think about a drop, the idea that you will get is of a drop of the ocean and as a result you will disappear like others without making any mark in life. But if you think about the ocean, the ideas that you will get shall be much bigger than those droplet ideas.

How do we do it?

Your aim should be in cognizance with that of the world. Bill Gates wanted to see a computer at every desk. He wanted to see people using it as he understood how computers can simplify life and unite the huge world. He had his interests in computers and as a result he did not make it big only for himself but for the entire world by revolutionising the needs of the world.

You should be ready to sacrifice your interests for the world. Your interests do not mean your goal or aim of life. Also, I am not asking you to sacrifice your interests because your parents, spouse, girlfriend, or society want it. Sacrificing of interests means that you are willing to sacrifice your need and desires for something bigger, bend down against others' ego, not think about yourself and continue to work towards what you are and wish to do always, keeping in mind the bigger interests of the world than your own. The sacrifice does not also mean to sacrifice your area of interest or potential. "The harder I work, the more I will earn and the more I earn the more tax I will pay. Hence, more money shall be used for the world and the nation".

You should be willing to go to any extent to realize your dream. That is the reason houses are made of bricks today. It is because people have strong desires and expectations from life and they continue working towards it and keep promising the family members that they are doing it only for them.

You should be prepared not to run but face the unexpected challenges. We have all heard this many times and we are hearing it once again. But in spite of reading this, when the time to show our courage and face comes, we tend to show the symptoms of irritation, avoidance, and evasiveness as if we are disinterested. But the fact is that we are not disinterested as our impulsive calculation shows that we cannot come out of it, so we pretend being disinterested.

Knowing is not enough. If we know what, when and why to do something, it is as good as not knowing if you do not implement it perfectly. We often feel guilty within us about things we know, we should have done but we don't. At that time no matter what we do or believe or put an excuse to convince ourselves that we have taken a right/ appropriate decision but the fact still remains that we are not fooling others but we are fooling ourselves, hence we can be responsible to ourselves. Similarly, we can also be responsible to the world but since it does not effect us directly hence, we think it is not important.

Ask yourself how nationalistic are you, also whether you are a real nationalist or a disguised nationalist by answering the following questions:

Name five things which you think this world is not sincere about?

_____
_____
_____
_____
_____

What things are we lacking as a nation?

_____
_____
_____
_____
_____

Channelizing Self for Success

How do you think we can change it? Please be specific?

_____

_____

_____

_____

How do you think you can contribute to changing the world and your nation?

Make specific promises.

_____

_____

_____

_____

❑❑❑

MIND COACH

"The Nutrition for your Mind"
Mind Coach Mobile Software for Rs. 699/- only

Free

> Software upgrade for 1 year
> +
> Motivational quotes every week for 3 months
> +
> 2 Books : Secrets of Success & Channelizing Self for Success

Mind Coach is a software invented by Dr. Kapil Kakar. Through scientifically researched psychological questions and answers, it helps to confront and regenerate the unpleasant emotions into desired positive behavior. Mind Coach deals with emotions such as Stress, Fear, Anxiety, Decision making, Anger, Uncertainty and more. It can be run on a mobile phone as well as an exclusive Mind Coach hand-held Device.

INSTITUTE OF PERSONALITY STRESS SPIRITUALITY RESEARCH PVT. LTD.

E-33, Jangpura Extension
New Delhi-110014
Mobile: 9899999158
website: www.kapilkakar.com, www.corporatetrainingindia.net
Email: contact@kapilkakar.com

PERSONALITY DEVELOPMENT

4th Idiot
Author : B. R. Chowdhary
Rs. 150

Memory Mind & Body
Author : B. R. Chowdhary
Rs. 195

Memorising Dictionary Made Easy
Author : B. R. Chowdhary
Rs. 150

Impossible... Possible...
Author : B. R. Chowdhary
Rs. 150

Memory Unlimited
Author : B. R. Chowdhary
Rs. 150

Dynamic Memory Methods
Author: B. R. Chowdhary
Rs. 150

Vocabulary @ 100 words/Hr.
Author: B. R. Chowdhary
Rs. 95

One Minute Memory Mind Manager
Author : B. R. Chowdhary
Rs. 75

Turn Your Creative Spark Into a Flame
Author: Joginder Singh
Rs. 95

How To Excel When Chips Are Down
Author : Joginder Singh
Rs. 150

Winning Ways
Author : Joginder Singh
Rs. 150

Success Mantra
Author : Joginder Singh
Rs. 150

For A Better Tomorrow
Author: Joginder Singh
Rs. 150

Nothing is Impossible
Author : Joginder Singh
Rs.150

Think Big Become Big
Author : Tarun Engineer
Rs. 150

Memory Techniques For science students
Author : N. Roy Chowdhury
Rs. 95

DIAMOND BOOKS X-30, Okhla Industrial Area, Phase-II, New Delhi-110020,
Phones : 41611861- 65, 40712700, Fax: 011- 41611866
E-mail : Sales@dpb.in, Website: www.dpb.in

PERSONALITY DEVELOPMENT

Yes You Can
Dr. Harikrishan Devsare
Rs. 95

Tips of Success
Sunil Jogi
Rs. 95

Science of Mind Simplified
B. K. Chandra Shekhar
Rs. 125

Invisible Doctor
B.K. Chandra Shekhar
Rs. 125

Nothing is Impossible
Author : Joginder Singh
Rs. 150

Learn To Say I Love You
Surya Sinha....Rs. 150

Unlock the Door to Success
Ashok Jain....Rs. 125

Come on! Get Set Go
Swati - Shailesh Lodha
Rs. 195

Why Women Are What They Are
Swati Lodha....Rs. 195

The Excellence In You
Dr. Giriraj Shah
Rs. 150

The Secret of Happiness
Jas Mand....Rs. 195

Memory Techniques For science students
N. Roy Chowdhury....Rs. 95

A guide to Network Marketing
Surya Sinha....Rs. 100

Beat Exam The Smart Way
Dr. Sunil Vaid....Rs. 150

Success in Exams
Vijay Anand
Rs. 75

Sure Success In Interviews
Tarun Chakarborty....Rs. 95

DIAMOND BOOKS
X-30, Okhla Industrial Area, Phase-II, New Delhi-110020.
Phones : 41611861- 65, 40712100, Fax: 011- 41611866
E-mail : Sales@dpb.in, Website: www.dpb.in

PERSONALITY DEVELOPMENT

Management Guru Bhagwan Shri Ram
Dr. Sunil Jogi....Rs. 95

Management Guru Hanuman
Dr. Sunil Jogi....Rs. 95

Secrets Of Success Through Bhagwadgeeta
Kapil Kakkar....Rs. 95

Management Guru Chankya
Himanshu Shekha....Rs. 95

Management Guru Ganesha
B.K. Chandrashekhar
Rs. 125

Management Guru Professor Laloo's Rail
Dr. Sunil Jolgi....Rs. 150

Time Management
Dr. Rakha Vyas
Rs. 125

Be An Achiever
K G Varshney
Rs. 95

Gandhi and Management
Dr. Pravin Shukl....Rs. 95

Think And Grow Rich
Napoleon Hill
Rs. 100

Golden Sutra Of Success
P. Gopal Sharma
Rs. 95

Dare to Dream Dare to Excel
Dr. H. Devsre....Rs. 95

Power of Positive Thinking
G.D.Budhiraja....Rs. 95

Power to Write your Own Desting
Ashok Indu....Rs. 125

Success Is Not By Chance
Ashok Indu....Rs. 95

Think Big Become Big
Tarun Engineer....Rs. 150

DIAMOND BOOKS
X-30, Okhla Industrial Area, Phase-II, New Delhi-110020,
Phones : 41611861- 65, 40712600, Fax: 011- 41611866
E-mail : Sales@dpb.in, Website: www.dpb.in